CURIOSITIES FROM THE CABINET

Objects and Voices from
Britain's Museums

Rebecca Reynolds

Curiosities from the Cabinet
Objects and Voices from Britain's Museums
Written by Rebecca Reynolds
Illustrations by Minho Kwon

© Rebecca Reynolds 2016
All rights reserved

Published in 2016 by Finca Press
ISBN: 978-0-9955167-0-0 (Trade Paperback)
ISBN: 978-0-9955167-1-7 (Kindle/Mobi)
ISBN: 978-0-9955167-2-4 (ePub)

Cover design by Dan Mogford
Page layout by Lighthouse24

For my family

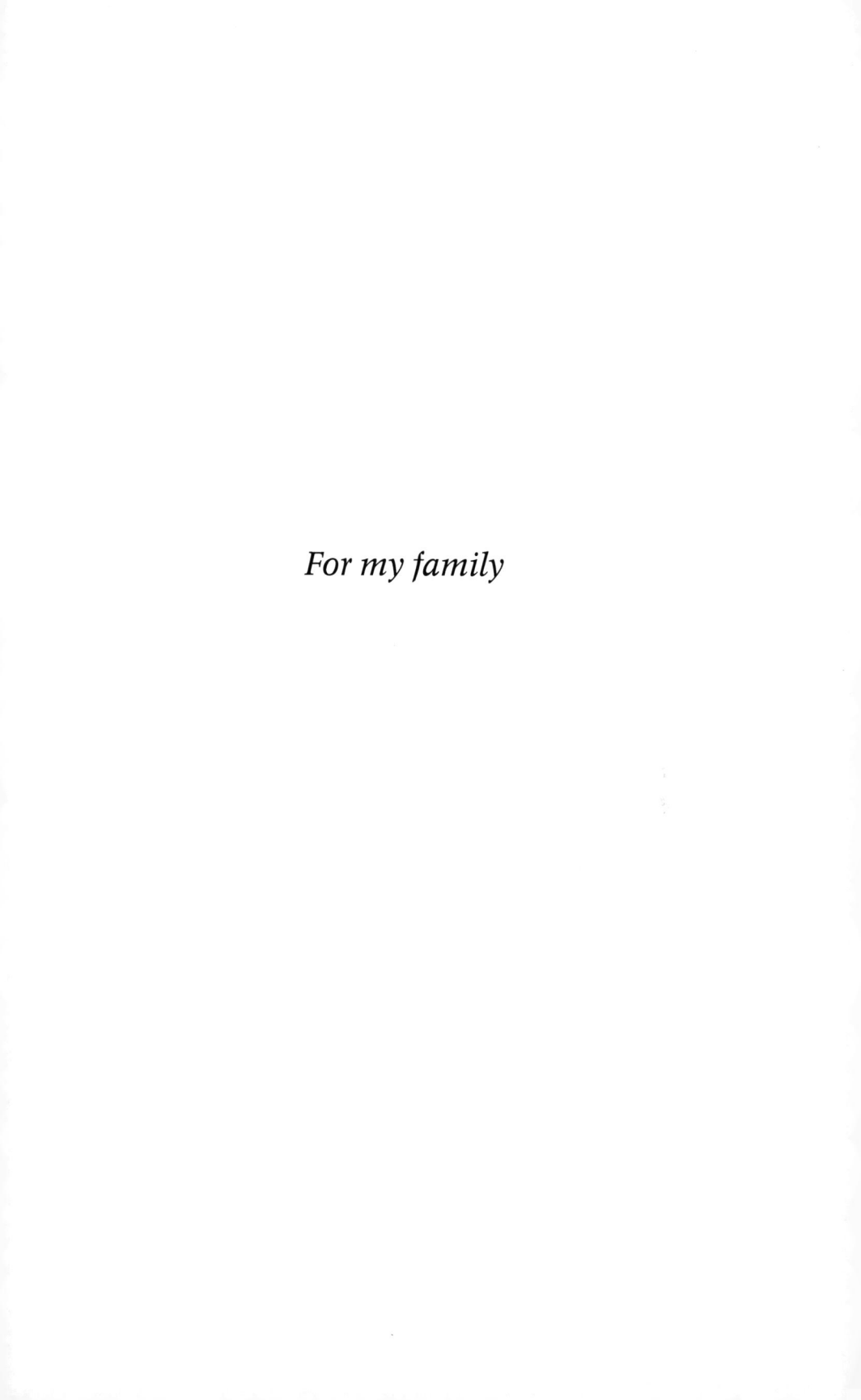

Contents

Introduction: Opening the Cabinet   1

Inside the Cabinet

THE TOUCHABLE   8
- Quilt   11
  St Fagans Museum
- Bastet figurine   14
  Petrie Museum of Egyptian Archaeology
- Souvenir anointing spoon   18
  Royal Historic Palaces online gift shop

THE RECREATED   23
- Casts of Parthenon Sculptures   25
  Elgin Museum
- Colossus rebuild   28
  National Museum of Computing
- Lucifer   32
  Birmingham Museum and Art Gallery

THE EPHEMERAL	39
Mermaid flyer	41
Centre for Ephemera Studies	
Toilet paper	44
Land of Lost Content	
Twitter feed	49
The British Library	
THE LETHAL	55
Mercury	57
Ulster Museum	
Flintlock pistols	60
Kelvingrove Art Gallery and Museum	
Euthanasia machine	63
Science Museum	
THE DEAD	69
Barn owl	70
Booth Museum	
Crocodile handbag	72
Cole Museum of Zoology	
Jeremy Bentham auto-icon	74
University College London	
THE LIVING	79
Leafcutter ants	81
Liverpool World Museum	
Darwin's weed garden	84
Down House	
Captain Woodget	88
The Cutty Sark	

THE EXTINCT	93
Quagga skeleton	96
Grant Museum of Zoology	
Babylonian map of the world	100
British Museum	
Bends used for peat flittin'	105
Fetlar Interpretive Centre	
THE MOBILE	111
Skeleton marionette	112
Victoria and Albert Museum	
Wave machine	115
Whipple Museum of the History of Science	
Brantly B2B helicopter	120
Helicopter Museum	
THE VERBAL	124
Paradise Lost	126
Milton's Cottage	
Wesley monument	130
Museum of London	
Probate copy of the will of Thomas Leyland	133
International Slavery Museum	
THE DOMESTIC	138
Britains toy farm set	139
Museum of English Rural Life	
Homemaker plate	141
Brighton Museum and Art Gallery	
Jane Austen's writing table	146
Jane Austen's House Museum	

THE HUGE	151
Coal mine	152
Big Pit National Coal Museum	
Emigrant sailing ship	157
Ulster American Folk Park	
Monasterboice cross	161
Victoria and Albert Museum	
THE CURIOUS	164
Hans Sloane's specimen tray	166
British Museum	
Powhatan's mantle	168
Ashmolean Museum of Art and Archaeology	
The Vegetable Lamb of Tartary	172
The Garden Museum	
Closing the Cabinet	176
References and further resources	183
List of museums	196
Acknowledgements	202
Copyright and permissions	203
About the author	205
About the artist	205

Introduction:
Opening the Cabinet

IN THE BRITISH MUSEUM'S Enlightenment Gallery you can find the Chaucer stone, a piece of flint broken open to show the shape of the poet's face. Oxford's Ashmolean Museum displays Powhatan's Mantle, a large piece of shell-decorated leather procured from native American Indians in the 17th century, said to have belonged to the father of Princess Pocahontas. The Natural History Museum in South Kensington displays a nautilus shell minutely carved with cherubs and golden fronds.

All these are survivors from the earliest cabinets of curiosities, kept throughout Europe in the 16th and 17th centuries. The cabinet could be either a room or a cupboard; the curiosities were objects for studying or showing to visitors. By collecting and ordering them, one could understand the world, and indeed some cabinets tried to recreate the world in microcosm. A visitor to gardener and collector John Tradescant's cabinet in 1634 said it was a place 'where a Man might in one daye behold and collecte into one place more curiosities than hee should see if hee spent all his life in Travell'.

Collectors could be physicians, naturalists, explorers or wealthy amateurs. Outside Britain they were often members of the aristocracy or royalty. Objects in the cabinets could be man-made or natural, and – though mainly collected for study purposes – were often wonderfully weird: as well as the Chaucer stone, physician Hans Sloane's collection contained a medical specimen tray with a mummy's finger and rhinoceros horn. Gustavus Adolphus's Kunstschrank, which can still be seen in the University of Uppsala's Gustavianum Museum in Sweden, contains joke items such as fake food and 'vexing spectacles'.

Two contemporary descriptions of cabinets help us to explore these early collections. In 1594 the English writer Francis Bacon described the ideal possessions of a prince:

> First, the collecting of a most perfect and general library, wherein whosoever the wit of man hath heretofore committed to books of worth…may be contributory to your wisdom. Next, a spacious, wonderful garden, wherein whatsoever plant the sun of divers climate, or the earth out of diverse moulds, either wild or by the culture of man brought forth, may be…set and cherished: this garden to be built about with rooms to stable in all rare beasts and to cage in all rare birds; with two lakes adjoining, the one of freshwater the other of salt, for like variety of fishes. And so you have in small compass the model of the universal nature made private. The third, a goodly huge cabinet wherein whatsoever the hand of man by exquisite art or engine has made rare in stuff, form or motion; whatsoever singularity, chance, and the shuffle of things has produced; whatsoever nature has wrought in things that want life and may be kept; shall be sorted and included. The fourth such a still house, so furnished with mills, instruments, furnaces and vessels as may be a palace fit for a philosopher's stone.

So the cabinet takes its place within a mini-universe, which like an ark contains all animals and birds, as well as plants. Bacon wants everything systematised and ordered here – 'the model of the universal nature made private'. But that wonderfully concrete phrase 'the shuffle of things', which the cabinet will display, implies there is unavoidable randomness in its contents.

In early descriptions of these cabinets by their visitors or owners what you have, above all, are lists – long, lovely, unhierarchical lists which take pleasure in displaying these objects to the reader through language. When diarist John Evelyn visited the Ruzzini Collection in Venice in 1645, 50 years later than Bacon's description of the ideal cabinet, he wrote:

> On Michaelmas day I went with my Lord Mowbray (eldest son to the Earle of Arundell & most worthy Person) to see the Collection of a Noble Venetian Signor Rugini: he has a stately Palace, richly furnish'd, with statues, heads of the Roman Empp, which are all plac'd in an ample room: In the next was a Cabinet of Medals in both Latine and Greeke, with divers curious shells, & to faire Pearles in 2 of them: but above all, he abounded in things petrified, Walnuts, Eggs, in which the Yealk rattl'd, a Peare, a piece of beefe, with the bones in it; an whole hedg-hog, a plaice on a Wooden Trencher turned into Stone, and very perfect... In another Cabinet... he shew'd us several Intaglias, of Achat, especially a Tiberius's head, & a Woman in a Bath with her dog: Some rare Cornelians, Onixes Chrystals &c in one of which was a drop of Water not Congeal'd but plainly moving up & down... then he shew'd us divers pieces of Amber wherein were several Insects intomb'd, in particular one cut like an heart, that contain'd [in] it a Salamander, without the least defect; & many curious pieces of Mosaic:

It is as though Evelyn is lost in these objects like rooms within rooms, or drawers within drawers. It is an experience not unlike getting lost in the galleries of a large museum.

And indeed the germs of some of today's grand national museums were in these collections, when they were donated to the state to use for wider benefit. Hans Sloane's collection started the British Museum when it was founded in 1753. Sloane said in his will that by expanding knowledge of the works of nature, his collection would 'raise our ideas' of the 'perfections of the Deity'. Elias Ashmole donated the collections of the royal gardeners, the Tradescant father and son, to the University of Oxford in 1677, stating that in order to understand nature, studying specimens was essential.

How did those early collectors and visitors look at and use these curiosities? What went through their minds as they explored the surprising and wonderful forms in front of them? When the Royal Society was founded in 1660 by physicians and natural philosophers, one of its aims was to compile a comprehensive collection, which would make it easy 'to find likenesse and unlikenesse of things upon a suddaine'. Modern commentators speak of collectors looking at 'the play of analogies, correspondences and resemblances' and 'curious juxtapositions'.

Collectors focused very much on the actual objects and their physical properties; catalogues rarely contain detailed acknowledgements of the environments which objects came from or (if they were plant or animal remains) of how other organisms may have interacted with them. However, John Tradescant the younger wrote about examining the materials in his collection and assessing 'the agreements with severall Authors', mentioning both ancient and contemporary writers including Aristotle, the natural philosopher Pliny the Elder, and the 16th-century European naturalists Aldrovandi and Rondelet.

Today's museums are more ordered than those early cabinets. Displays may be arranged according to carefully considered themes, often with multimedia interpretation and planned routes for visitors to follow. Yet I wonder if some visitors do not feel some nostalgia for piles of uninterpreted objects yielding chance discoveries, perhaps disordered heaps of gemstones or bones remembered from childhood museum visits. For objects often resist being managed into coherent stories and collecting always has a chance element. And so museums are witnesses to the partial nature of physical evidence and the incomplete state of our knowledge about the world.

This book is a small cabinet in words, with something of the delight in detail of Evelyn's description. Early cabinets of curiosities sometimes classified their objects as natural or man-made. In this one you will find categories such as 'the extinct', 'the huge', 'the lethal'. Objects from the original cabinets are there, including Hans Sloane's medical samples and Powhatan's mantle.

As in Bacon's cabinet, there are objects made by nature and by man. They come from natural history, art and design, agriculture, engineering, and other areas. The selection also shows something of Bacon's 'shuffle of things'. For example, the quagga was alive in Bacon's time but is now in 'the extinct' section – although in the future we may be able to bring extinct animals back to life through their DNA, as the curator of the museum holding the quagga skeleton explains. Instead of Bacon's 'rare birds' there is the homely barn owl, the one in this book found dead on the road and stuffed.

But 'curiosity' is a feeling as well as a thing, and this book is about people as much as objects. Although labelled and behind glass, museum objects are the bearers of people's thoughts, feelings and actions over decades and centuries. And there are also the people who love, care for and know about the objects once they have entered the museum – curators, conservators and educators. So in the book, alongside the objects, are the voices of these 'museum insiders' who know the objects intimately. These speakers often touch on what they think the purposes of museums are too.

We also hear from people outside the museum world – donors, visitors, academics, whose more varied interpretations do not often appear in museum displays. But these people offer other perspectives, showing effects which objects can have on people's thoughts and feelings. These contributions take different forms – stories, mini-lectures, reminiscences. For example, retired woman Philippa Hughes speaks about making imaginary farms on her bedroom floor as a child with the toy animals she gave to a rural life museum, and microbiologist Andrew Lilley describes how seeing a euthanasia machine helped clarify his thoughts about the right to die.

Lastly, these objects reveal how various museums are – the poet John Milton's cottage in the small village of Chalfont St Giles in Buckinghamshire; the vast shiny Science Museum in London; the Booth Museum in Brighton, packed floor-to-ceiling with stuffed specimens, itself almost a relic. Researching and writing this book has been an exciting voyage of discovery. From learning that friends of the philosopher Jeremy Bentham probably socialised with his clothed skeleton after he had died, to hearing about the dedicated rebuilding of the Colossus World War II codebreaking computer, I was amazed to learn about some of the stories which start with objects in our museums.

This book arose from questions I found myself asking when I started working in museums, based at London's Victoria and Albert Museum as a teacher and education researcher, mainly working with art and design undergraduates. During this time I found myself in a world where objects, not words, ruled – not only inside the museum itself, but also in the ways in which design students and tutors thought and practised. As someone who had always been drawn to words and to reading, this was quite foreign to me.

So to investigate ways in which people saw, valued and thought about objects I carefully chose museum objects from around the country and recorded people, from both inside and outside museums, speaking about them. Five years later, I ended up with a range of ways of understanding objects – 'a kaleidoscope of voices', as a colleague put it – as well as knowledge about the objects themselves. A cabinet of curiosity seemed a natural way of recognising the disparate nature of these contributions, while imposing some minimal order on them. I have also tried to stay with individual objects for as long as possible, rather than trying to trace connections between them or making them part of a larger story.

Like museums, the book is browsable, and you may wish to follow it from start to finish or pick and choose objects which catch your eye. It is not a book of highlights or a guide, but may act as a prompt to the reader to follow their own curiosity in exploring further, through the range of resources which museums now offer, from displays and exhibitions, to archives and libraries, to the growing number of events which museums run. Ways of doing this are indicated at the back of the book, where there are addresses and websites of the museums, along with suggestions for further reading and looking.

Inside the Cabinet

The Touchable

IN MUSEUMS we are both dazzled and deprived. Dazzled with a rich, informative environment full of rarities, set up to capture our attention. Deprived, because we have to rely almost exclusively on the sense of sight. This changes the way we understand objects – musical instruments are seen but not played or heard; carpets are not walked on; hardly anything is smelt or tasted. We admire the appearance of a sofa rather than check how comfortable it is; we observe the structure of a skeleton rather than feel the strength of the bones. Fabrics can't be felt on the skin or knife blades tested.

But touch is important, allowing us to appreciate attributes such as weight and wear properly. Fingertips seek imperfections and marks left by previous owners. People with visual impairments rely on touch, and children instinctively grab in order to investigate.

Touch also suggests intimacy and possession. 'Don't squeeze me till I'm yours!' says the mildly saucy greengrocer's sign on fruit and vegetables. You control an object in your hand and do not have to rely on the way it has been presented to you. You can turn it, examine its concealed angles, choose the parts of it you want to explore. It becomes a more private experience than looking at it through glass.

In fact, objects were often handled in early museums. Celia Fiennes, a visitor to the Ashmolean Museum in about 1694, reported: 'there is a Cane which looks like a solid heavy thing but if you take it in your hands it's as light as a feather', and as late as 1827 the Ashmolean regulations allowed visitors to handle objects with the curator's permission. A German traveller, Sophie de la Roche, wrote ecstatically about a visit to the British Museum in 1786:

> With what sensations one handles a Carthaginian helmet excavated near Capua, household utensils from Herculaneum... There are mirrors too, belonging to Roman matrons... with one of these mirrors in my hand I looked amongst the urns, thinking meanwhile, 'Maybe chance has preserved amongst these remains some part of the dust from the fine eyes of a Greek or Roman lady, who so many centuries ago surveyed herself in this mirror...' Nor could I restrain my desire to touch the ashes of an urn on which a female figure was being mourned. I felt it gently, with great feeling... I pressed the grain of dust between my fingers tenderly, just as her best friend might once have grasped her hand...

For this visitor touch unlocked an intimacy which sight alone could not.

However, with changes in scientific practice in the 19th century, such as an increasing reliance on microscopes and measurement, sight took precedence over touch when investigating objects. In addition, curators needed to protect objects more diligently from the hands of increasing numbers of visitors.

Still, many museums recognise that sight is not enough and keep handling collections or 'touch exhibits'– even today, corsets can be squeezed into, handaxes wielded, stuffed animals stroked. But touch in museums is gentle and supervised. Objects cannot usually be taken apart or taken outside. Nevertheless, visitors often touch very attentively when invited to do so, perhaps because the experience is rationed. Touching itself can be reverential; I remember an exhibition of designs by the Italian fashion designer Gianni Versace in the Victoria and Albert Museum some years ago, at the end of which some touchable clothes were displayed. We obediently formed a line and shuffled forward, one by one feeling the hems of the garments as though they were holy relics.

Touch has a different role in relation to each of the three objects in this section. The first is a bed cover which quilters have to touch to understand how it was made. The second, a figurine made two and a half millennia ago, was taken to hospital bedsides for patients to handle for therapeutic purposes.

The third is an £8.99 souvenir replica of the anointing spoon from the Crown Jewels, which can be touched and possessed by anyone who can afford it. We all understand shop goods, and touch them unhesitatingly. The museum, however, is a more unusual context for objects. So objects in museum shops become a bridge between the everyday world of the high street and the more mysterious world of the museum, where the goods on display may not be bought.

QUILT

St Fagans Museum, Cardiff

FRENCH SCHOOLCHILDREN poke their heads inside recreated Welsh farm buildings from the 12th to the 20th century in the green, wooded grounds of St Fagans Museum. Water wheels turn on the flour and wool mills, and cakes are bought at the bakehouse. In the museum's light glass-walled library, textiles curator Elen Phillips unrolls a pale blue bedcover onto a table.

The museum has over 200 quilts from the 18th to the 20th centuries, of which about 20 are in the handling collection. Quilting used to be a popular cottage industry in Wales, and itinerant quilters would go from farm to farm with a quilting frame. This industry died out in the 1930s and the National Museum of Wales, of which St Fagans is now a part, 'went at it', as Elen puts it, collecting three or four quilts a year in an attempt to record traditional arts and crafts.

The pale blue quilt is one of Elen's favourites. Here she explains how and why it was made, describes why she is drawn to it and says why she thinks quilts should be handled.

> This wholecloth quilt was made by a woman called Winifred Williams in a class in a Working Men's Hall in Maerdy in the Rhondda, South Wales, taught by a teacher who worked at the Maes-yr-Haf Quaker settlement at Trealaw, also in the Rhondda. Maes-yr-Haf was a Victorian villa bought by the Quakers to teach craft and other skills to people who were suffering in the late 20s and 30s because of the economic depression. This was the devil's decade – the effect of the depression in Wales has been compared by some historians to that of the famine in Ireland.

Blankets, other quilts or even clothes could be sewn into new coverings. Wholecloth means that the quilt is made from an entire piece of fabric – like a textile sandwich – rather than pieces being stitched together. There is often a central roundel and perhaps spirals, veined leaves and hearts. Williams would have made the pattern up herself, and would have needed some mathematical ability to work out the geometry and balance of the design.

All quilts have a hidden layer. By touching you can understand the construction, layering, texture – with textiles it's all about touch. I guess it's the closest thing to using it. Folding, handling, caressing it – people do caress, they tend to stroke it a bit like an animal and feel the grooves, texture, 3D quality of the quilting. It's one step from sleeping under it.

Quilters by their very nature tend to want to grab things in museum displays and they love to count the stitches per inch, examine the finish, see areas of loss, guess what the filling would be. Having said that, even when we've gone through the rigmarole of washing hands, one or two participants in groups are always quite reticent to handle. They still stand miles from the table and won't touch and you've got to coax them closer.

Technically and aesthetically this is probably one of the least exciting quilts in the collection. The stitches are huge in comparison with those made by quilters today. It might even be her first quilt. But because of that it's less intimidating and more accessible.

Museums tend to showcase the best of everything, but in fact it's important to show different levels of skill. Here it's a museum about people, so really the quality of the work shouldn't matter, it should always be the story of the person behind the making. One of our remits here is to encourage a new generation of young people interested in craft; so we have to show them an entry level quilt.

It's also the story of the people that makes me tick as a curator. I'm from an industrial working class town in North East Wales which is dotted with Working Men's Halls, so it's representative of a Wales of my background as well.

The quilts are important and complex objects which the St Fagans of the future will not be interpreting purely as examples of Welsh crafts; we'll be placing them more in the political and social context. Rather than an example of women's handiwork, a quilt such as this can be seen as part of the story of the making of Wales as a nation.

Ann Rippin, Reader in the Department of Management at Bristol University, describes herself as an 'academic quilter'. She talked about a visit to see and touch the St Fagans quilts with the Bristol Quilters.

I use quilts to communicate research findings – for example, about organisations I've been looking at. I respond to a text and invite other people to respond by making and decorating quilts. Traditional academic papers are fine, but it was only when I started using art-based methods to present findings that people really took notice.

The sheer abundance of quilts at the museum is wonderful. The Welsh ones are woolly so you get deep shadows because of the stitching, which makes more of a crevice, which is inviting to explore. I was most interested in ones with worked-through edges, signs of wear which means you can see the previous quilt underneath. It has a honeycomb effect.

But haptic pleasure is difficult to put into words. I think touching is different in the museum – it's more respectful. There is a contrast between being invited to gaze and an invitation to touch. When you are gazing, the object is out of reach. But by handling it, you possess it temporarily, you are halfway there.

BASTET FIGURINE

Petrie Museum, London

THE SMALL BROWN FIGURINE of a cat lies in the palm of my hand, like a toy from a Christmas cracker. It is 7½ cm long, bronze, and made between 650 and 500 BC. The cat holds a basket of kittens and a sacred rattle, or sistrum, over one shoulder. The surface of the figurine is rough, but shinier on the face and basket, perhaps where it has been touched or rubbed more, and it shows some verdigris (from exposure to oxygen) in places.

Bastet was an Egyptian cat goddess and daughter of the sun god Ra. She was the goddess of the moon, sunrise, music, dance and pleasure as well as family, fertility and birth. Women in Ancient Egypt wanting children sometimes wore a Bastet amulet.

This figurine was taken to hospital bedsides by staff at University College London (UCL) along with other objects such as a fossil ammonite and an Iron Age flint axe head. In some of the first research of its kind, they wanted to find out if patients' well-being improved after they had handled museum objects.

Researchers invited patients to choose an object and talked to the patient while they explored and handled it, often telling them about it and asking about any thoughts or feelings which were evoked. The participants handled the objects in many different ways. They stroked and petted, touched hesitantly or absentmindedly, pulled the object close to themselves, worked it as it might originally have been used (for example, grabbing a dagger and making stabbing motions), and sometimes handled the object roughly.

Patients said they felt happier and the results showed that their well-being increased after touching the objects. In one study responses from a group of patients who had handled objects indicated greater improvements in well-being compared to responses from another group of patients who only looked at the pictures of the same selection of objects.

As well as wanting to know more about the artefacts' history, participants often associated them with aspects of their own lives. One woman facing cancer is quoted in an article describing why she had chosen Bastet:

> I am sure whoever made this didn't know…that this would be nestling in my hand, I suppose it makes me think perhaps that odd things I've done or people I've touched, in times to come I may have influenced them…nothing tangible like this to leave, but a legacy, nonetheless…
>
> Yes, I think that's the other thing that attracted me, is the rattle. There's a 'don't mess with me' you know as well, a quirkiness that I like…The reflection that in various aspects of my life I have been a powerful woman like her I had influence in the Union – there's a bit of me there.

Another, when told how old Bastet was, said that she had to hold it again and grasped it close, exclaiming 'Now I've been there by proxy!' Yet another tried to hide her at the end of the session.

The researchers comment that 'the object can act as a repository or container for projections of different and difficult states of mind. They have a particular valence for representing loss, because in order to bear loss we search for ways of finding the lost person, or, in the case of cancer patients, the loss of the healthy self. The object can therefore represent wholeness and integration.' They say that objects such as Bastet, which 'embodied a huge span of time and reached far into mankind's past as a link with human beings' genesis and universality' were crucial in evoking emotional responses and provided more than a present-day artefact could.

They have since found that other groups of people undergoing medical treatment, such as mental health patients and people recovering from addictions, report improvements in their own well-being after handling museum objects, although it is not clear how long these improvements last. The researchers would like to investigate whether learning new things shortens hospital stays or medication levels, and whether 'an aesthetic experience' with a museum object can lessen pain.

Helen Chatterjee, Professor of Biology at UCL, led the research. She spoke about Bastet's role in it:

> When I started this research I went to all the UCL museum curators and I said 'Please can you loan me objects I can take out to hospitals and care homes?', and this is one of the things the Petrie Museum of Egyptian Archaeology gave me. And instantly I thought 'Brilliant, this is going to be a really nice object because she's pretty, she's small, she fits in the palm of your hand, and she's got this interesting history and symbolic and protective functions.'
>
> As the researchers started running object handling sessions with patients, collecting data and reciting their stories, and when I ran some sessions, I realised that a lot of people were really drawn to Bastet for the same reasons that I was,

and some of the very interesting conversations often happened around her.

In one project, we were working with colleagues from the UCL Institute for Women's Health. The researchers were working with women who had cancer or were being screened for cancer.

They made some interesting findings about how women in particular related to Bastet. They found that handling the object enabled women to engage with talking about how their illness or the prospect of an illness had affected them psychologically, including some who had not done so before. We also connected this with research by Winnicott into how certain objects can mark a transition for us between our inner world and an outer reality which can be hard to deal with, and by Vygotsky, who says that the physicality of objects helps you discover and deal with emotions, particularly loss or bereavement.

Also the age thing comes up a lot – not just with Bastet but with fossils, say when you hand someone an ammonite that's 30 million years old. Someone said 'you can't feel depressed when you're holding something this old' and you can understand what they mean – I think what they are trying to say is it puts your life in context. The privilege thing has come out too – a lot of people will say 'it's made me feel special'. But the converse of that – to be fair – is that a small number of people have said that they don't feel that museums should be taking out collections and allowing people to touch them.

We got some negativity on the clinical side at first because lots of people think arts and health is total nonsense. Our point is that museums have an amazing array of collections, a lot are inaccessible, so if it can help people even psychologically then surely that is of benefit and is interesting to explore from a research perspective.

I think museums should allow people to touch objects more, while acknowledging that some material isn't going to be suitable. People also need to teach an audience how to handle objects carefully. Actually we found that helped, because if you show that it's not some tat but something that is valued, then it adds to the sense of privilege. It is a privilege even if you are working in museums and are able to touch these materials, but I don't see why that should be restricted to curators and conservators. Collections are here for us and we should be thinking about benefits to society in the broadest sense.

SOUVENIR ANOINTING SPOON

Royal Historic Palaces online gift shop

THE RETAIL CUSTOMER SERVICES TEAM at Historic Royal Palaces Enterprises Ltd tells me that the souvenir anointing spoon sells well, although they won't disclose figures. Costing £8.99, it comes in a plastic box with a card showing portraits of Elizabeth I, Victoria and Edward VII and is lead-free pewter plated with 22 carat gold. Like the real spoon, its bowl has a ridge down the centre and a pattern of acanthus scrolls. But at 11 centimetres long it is less than half the size of the original and is missing the original's pearls, stylised monster's heads and delicate, interlaced patterns. It is slightly lighter than a normal teaspoon, and bendable.

The real anointing spoon, part of the Crown Jewels, has been used in every coronation ceremony since that of James I in 1603. During the ceremony, holy oil is poured into the spoon from the ampulla, or vessel, shaped like a golden eagle. The Archbishop of Canterbury or officiating bishop then dips their fingers in the oil and anoints the new monarch's head, chest and hands.

The real spoon is a remarkable survival. It is first recorded in 1349 among St Edward's Regalia (older Crown Jewels) in Westminster Abbey, already described then as having 'antique forme'. It escaped being melted down by Oliver Cromwell in 1649 (unlike most of the Crown Jewels) and was sold to a Mr Kynnersley, Yeoman of Charles I's Wardrobe, for 16 shillings. Kynnersley returned the spoon to Charles II, for use at his coronation in 1661. However, it does not seem to have featured in Thomas Blood's attempt to steal the jewels from the Tower of London in 1671.

Anointing was one of the medieval holy sacraments, and goes back to the Old Testament, where Zadok the Priest and Nathan the Prophet anoint Solomon. Until the 17th century the sovereign was considered to be appointed directly by God, and coronation still confirms the monarch as the Head of the Church of England. The spoon is thus a strong symbol of the legitimacy, longevity and religious aspect of the monarchy.

Does the souvenir spoon retain any of this significance? Perhaps it could even lend itself to more imaginative, politically-charged interpretations – a symbol of oppression by the aristocracy and the church which people willingly buy and take into their own homes; a commodification of the monarchy; a satire on luxury objects; or even an object in its own right, telling a story as valid as its original.

Verity Hunt is an English lecturer at Southampton University with an interest in souvenirs and miniaturisation. She examined the spoon and shared her thoughts about it.

I guess what strikes me straight away is that it's just the size of a teaspoon, so it feels especially familiar. We're sitting here drinking tea and coffee, and straightaway it reminds you of that everyday object that you use through the day without thinking of it. But this is particularly ornate with the engravings and gilt colouring, so it's unfamiliar at the same time due to its decoration. It's pretty in a slightly kitsch way.

The miniaturisation is interesting. It's light and small, and lies easily in the palm of my hand. There's something about being able to wrap your whole hand around it, possess it entirely, which makes it particularly accessible.

You could just about imagine using it as a posh sugar spoon, to get out with your nicest china; you could fit a sugar lump on it, but it wouldn't work with loose sugar. Actually the design of it is a bit redundant; it's not the right shape for other purposes as soon as it's made smaller, which highlights the fact that it's not the size it should be. Not that your average tourist is going round anointing people!

Why would you buy it? Is it to make sense of a visit to the whole of the Crown Jewels at the Tower of London, which are quite overwhelming? It's ages since I've looked at them, but I remember this dazzling and visually chaotic mass of objects. Then this little one object that you purchase in the gift shop can somehow stand in and represent that confusing mass of things. And because it's something you take home, it becomes a tangible reminder of the Tower, like a link between that experience and your everyday life as it sits on your sideboard.

A souvenir can also become a trigger for a conversation, so if you'd shown that to family and friends it becomes a store for memory and a cue for reminiscing. It's partly about taking something monumental, the Coronation, which is this huge public state event with all the pomp that goes around that, and making it small and everyday and easier to read. The Crown Jewels are especially untouchable because of their huge financial value as well as their religious links.

It's democratising something that's priceless, in a way. It's secularising what is an especially elite object. You could say it's almost sacrilegious.

Lucifer
Birmingham Museum and Art Gallery

The Recreated

'Is it real?' is the question I am asked most often when I take groups of international students on museum trips. Objects in museums are trusted to be authentic, and to have everything that goes with this: validity as evidence, power to amaze, unique connections with different times and peoples.

But can reproductions possess qualities which the originals cannot? The philosopher Walter Benjamin thought so. Eighty years ago he argued that new reproduction techniques used with artworks posed a powerful challenge to cultural tradition. He agreed that the object's authority as historical evidence was undermined when that object was reproduced and that it lost the 'aura' that goes with authenticity. However, for him this had positive effects. Reproduction released great potential by creating multiple copies and enabling the viewer to see the object on their own terms: 'in permitting the reproduction to meet the beholder or listener in his own particular situation, it reactivates the object reproduced'.

The three objects in this section 'reactivate' the originals in different ways. The first is a miniature set of plaster casts of the Parthenon sculptures. The sculptures had been removed from the

Parthenon between 1801 and 1812 and brought to London by Lord Elgin, a move which was controversial from the beginning (Byron deplored their removal to 'northern climes abhorred' in his 1812 poem *Childe Harold's Pilgrimage*). Displayed in Piccadilly, they deeply impressed many people including the painter Benjamin Haydon and poet John Keats. Sculptor John Henning saw them in 1811, and was so struck that he spent years making tiny reproductions which came to the beholder, in Walter Benjamin's words, in 'their own particular situation' – not high on the Acropolis, but in the hands or on the mantelpieces of the owners.

The second is a rebuild of the Colossus Second World War code-breaking machine, the world's first electronic computer. All Colossi were destroyed after World War II to prevent any risk of their revolutionary decoding techniques falling into enemy hands. The rebuild gives us not only a reproduction of the machine, but a literal reactivation of the formulas and calculations which the original Colossi used. It has also recreated the process of putting the machine together – this took 11 months during World War II, but 14 years for the rebuild, using minimal surviving sources.

The third object is recreated by means of a subversive addition. Ceramicist Matt Smith added green carnations, a symbol of homosexuality, to a sculpture of fallen angel Lucifer. In his commentary on the statue, he explains why.

CASTS OF THE PARTHENON SCULPTURES

Elgin Museum, Elgin

'MR INGRAM WAS FREAKY but I loved it!' comments a seven-year-old in the Elgin Museum visitors' book. He is talking about a rather spooky mannequin of William Ingram, from 1836 the museum's first Keeper, which sits in a tower in this golden sandstone building in an attractive Scottish east coast town.

As well as objects carefully marshalled to tell the history of the local area, the museum houses curious artefacts from far-flung places, testimony to the pioneering and exploring instincts of the Scots. There is a shrunken head, or tsantsa, from Ecuador, and a 15th-century mummy stolen from Peru in the mid-19th century, crouched in the foetal position under a bell jar. Jutting out from the wall is a stag's head. This replaced the head of a white rhino shot in the Sudan in 1913 which had to be removed from the museum because of a spate of rhino horn thefts.

A history of local worthies also adorns the walls and there's a Jacob Epstein bust of former British Prime Minister Ramsay MacDonald, born in nearby Lossiemouth. Mementos of residents killed in the First World War are displayed alongside a gas mask and pith helmet, and there are stones and keys found around nearby Elgin Cathedral, now a ruin. The museum has its own local mummy – a cat found during restoration work in Greyfriars Convent opposite in 1895, probably the remains of a live one walled up for luck.

I had travelled to Elgin Museum hoping for an interesting story about how it came to acquire copies of the Elgin marbles. But in fact, the town only has a tenuous connection with the 7th Earl of Elgin who brought the marbles to Britain. Thomas Bruce, the first Earl of Elgin was given the title in 1633, probably as a reward from

King Charles I for contributing money to his coronation in Scotland. (Lord Bruce joked at the time that the English would at least be able to pronounce the name). However Bruce spent most of his time in England and his family home was elsewhere, in Fife.

The casts are in their own display case upstairs, near a Burmese Buddha from about 1800. They are tiny, like dominoes, and the pleats on the robes of the men and women are as thin as hairs. On this small scale the figures clearly emerge as one procession. A foxed card at the bottom of the case says they were donated by the Countess of Seafield in 1886.

It is difficult now to fully understand the excitement which the marbles created in those who first saw them in Britain. Benjamin Haydon visited them in 1808 in a 'critical agony of anxiety' about his painting of heroic Roman soldier Dentatus. The marbles helped him understand how to paint bodies in motion. 'When I saw... the most heroic style of art combined with all the essential detail of actual life the thing was done at once and for ever,' he wrote in his autobiography. '[I] saw the muscle showing under one armpit in that instantaneous action of darting out, and left out in the other armpits because not wanted.' He learnt that 'the end of the toes are the parts that are press[ed] down, the other joints not, consequently the flesh must rise all up about the nail, and the top of the upper joint keep its form.' Haydon thought, spoke and wrote about the sculptures for the rest of his life.

After John Henning saw them he started sculpting intricate slate moulds from which miniature reproductions of the marbles were made. At the same time he carved a mould of the Bassae frieze (parts of which are also in the British Museum), the whole project taking him 12 years. He hoped that the casts he could then produce from the moulds would repay him for this enormous investment of time, energy and skill. The resulting miniature Parthenon friezes were two inches high and 24 feet long, in tiles each eight inches long. The moulds are in the British Museum (and copies of the casts can be bought in its shop – the Charioteers set costs £11.99 – although they are not of a quality which Henning would have approved).

Vice-president of Elgin Museum Janet Trythall and Museum Assistant Heather Townsend told me more:

> Henning saw the Parthenon sculptures for the first time in 1811 in a makeshift museum on the corner of Park Lane and Piccadilly, just after Lord Elgin brought them to Britain. He was so impressed that he at once asked Lord Elgin for permission to draw them. The sculptures had been badly damaged in an explosion at the Parthenon in 1687, when it was used as a munitions store by the Turkish army and hit by a mortar fired by their enemies, the Venetians.
>
> Luckily a French artist, Jacques Carrey, had made drawings of them earlier, and Henning used these and other drawings to reconstruct the order of the procession and fill in details missing from the sculptures as he saw them. However, the reason why Henning went out of business, became a pauper essentially, is because this project was supposed to be an investment for life, but copies of his reproductions were then made all over the place without control.
>
> It's interesting how many noblemen and artists had copies of the frieze in their living room or dining room. Even if the Parthenon had survived various earthquakes, being used as a gunpowder store, the ravages of weather and time, you probably wouldn't in Athens have been able to see the detail, follow the story and understand the concept of what these figures are doing. In addition, the frieze was high up below the Parthenon's roof, so the ordinary visitor wouldn't have been able to see the story of the procession. To have copies on your table or in a cabinet to show people was a huge advantage.

The whole concept of making casts was a huge industry in the 19th century, and it brought the art to the people – it's accessible and stimulating. Now it's a good deal easier to get to London or even Greece than it would have been two hundred years ago.

It's very important that the museum has objects on display which link it to the Marbles. We occasionally get a visitor, fresh from a visit to the British Museum in London, who comes to Scotland looking for the Elgin Marbles. We used to have bags of marbles – or 'doolies' – in the shop as a consolation prize!

THE COLOSSUS REBUILD

The National Museum of Computing, Bletchley

AT FIRST SIGHT Bletchley Park near Milton Keynes looks like a small-scale, slightly run down business park, a collection of low huts with corrugated tile roofs spread over an estate with roads, mini-roundabouts and a pond. There are clues to its past as a World War II code-breaking centre – a group of secondary school children straggle past, tourists wearing cameras pause and look around, a model of a submarine rests outside one of the huts. For the site has been preserved, and visitors can now learn about the decrypting of German messages which played a crucial part in winning World War II, and see some of the machines used to do it.

The National Museum of Computing is in H block at the back of the site, a long low building. Exhibits inside go from huge mainframe computers to the latest mobile phones, along with more miscellaneous displays – a collection of slide rules, policy documents on IT education in schools. In the centre of its own room stands the Colossus rebuild, a rather naked assemblage of metal frames with rows of circuitry and computer valves resembling small light bulbs.

The original Colossus was the world's first electronic digital computer – the first to use electronic valves working together, rather than mechanical parts driven by electricity. It was built in 11 high-pressure months in 1943 by a team led by engineer Tommy Flowers, who had been a telecommunications worker at the General Post Office, and including mathematician Bill Tutte.

Colossus helped to decode messages from the German High Command, which were encrypted on a machine called the Lorenz. The Lorenz operators set its 12 wheels so that it would transform a message into code. These messages were intercepted when they were sent over the airwaves. Colossus then subjected them to a 'statistical attack' in order to find the starting positions of the 12 wheels, allowing the message to be read. It broke about 90% of messages, most in 4-6 hours.

Colossi were broken up after World War II, with many of the parts being used for telephone exchanges. But 50 years later a team of engineers set out to recreate the machine, led by Tony Sale, who had been a scientist for MI5 and had restored and curated computers at the Science Museum. Sale wanted to get on with the work while some of those who had worked on the Colossus during the war were still alive, so that they could contribute their memories, and he and his wife Margaret Sale initially funded the rebuild.

Part of Sale's motivation was that for too long the Americans had 'got away with the myth' that the ENIAC, a later computer, was the first large-scale electronic digital computer. Margaret Sale, who still works at the museum, and with her husband and others helped to preserve Bletchley Park, adds that the story of Colossus and the opportunity to do something worthwhile excited them. She mentions her late husband's 'sheer cussed streak' which meant he could not neglect the challenge.

At first there were only eight photographs and a few diagrams to work from, but in 1995 a breakthrough came with the release of a detailed technical description of Colossus which had been written by a US Army scientist visiting Bletchley during the war.

The last part went on the rebuild in 2004 and it is now run regularly in the museum. When it is turned on, paper tapes run around spools at 30 miles an hour at one end of the machine as the data is fed in. A regular clunk is heard as Colossus does its calculations and results are printed out on an electric typewriter. Four electric fires' worth of heat is emitted (Sale used to tell the story that the Wrens – members of the Women's Royal Naval Service – who operated the machine during World War II strung up a clothesline over it to dry their underwear).

Colossus chief engineer Phil Hayes describes his role as 'the ultimate job'. He came from a career in IT security, specialising in e-commerce for a major clearing bank in London, and started working on the project in 2000. After Sale's death in 2011 he took over running and researching the machine. He describes how the team approached the rebuild and says why seeing a working Colossus is important.

> A lot of information about Colossus is classified today because it uses very powerful statistical techniques. Breaking the Lorenz code without Colossus would take roughly 500,000 million years, because of the number of possible wheel combinations. Using a mathematical technique based on Bill Tutte's work, it was usually broken in 4-6 hours. There are other mathematical techniques connected with Colossus which are not in the public domain.

As far as we are aware, there are no Colossi left. There was no reason to keep them. To keep the algorithms – yes. To keep them a secret – yes. But not the machine.

Since there was hardly any documentation, a lot of the rebuild had to be reverse engineered. This means that you work backwards from information about the finished machine, to find out where particular parts go. So, for example, you are working on a part of the circuit that you want to fit on the machine. You've got a picture of the machine and you've got parts of a circuit diagram but you have no idea where your particular bit of circuit goes. So you count the number of valves on the bit of the circuit you're working on, go to the picture and try to locate a module which would have that number of valves. Then you put your circuit on the machine, then someone else will come along and put their modules on, and the piece you've been doing doesn't work any more. You are going forward three steps and going back two all the time.

What you're trying to do is get into the mindset of the engineers. I did this by using reference books, researching into Strowger switchgear and mechanical telephone systems.

Colossus works fully. There is only one real Lorenz machine which works – it's here at Bletchley Park in B block. This was shipped out to Germany in 2007 under armed guard for the international challenge, to decrypt a message which was transmitted out of Germany on the original Lorenz. This was picked up by radio at Bletchley and run through Colossus. It took about four hours for Colossus to find the starting positions. A German guy broke it in 47 seconds with powerful networked PCs and special software he'd written.

It's a rebuild and we are very protective of that. To be called a rebuild it has to meet certain criteria. Firstly, it must look the part, which it does because we've got photos of the originals to prove it. Secondly, everything must be of authentic type. Even though the relays were built in the 1960s, they are 3000 type relays, which is exactly what they used during the war. And thirdly, you must have one original component on the machine, and so we run one transformer from an original Mark II Colossus.

Colossus is run every day. You can see it running, you can hear it, you can feel the heat coming off it. We get Wrens visiting who worked here during World War II. One lady came in as part of a tour, and said she had worked on Colossus during the Second World War. She stood in front of the machine and said 'this is not Colossus'. I said 'Does it sound like it?' She said no. Then the electric typewriter connected to the machine started to print out. She instantly stopped, turned round, looked at the typewriter and said 'that's Colossus'. Because that was her job – she was responsible for the output of Colossus. The sound of the electric typewriter was what she remembered.

LUCIFER

Birmingham Museum and Art Gallery

LUCIFER GAZES DOWNWARDS, although he doesn't seem to see what is in front of him. His arms are stretched forward with wrists bent, as though he is falling, and one foot is slipping off his plinth. He has a muscular body and glorious extravagant wings, attached with a tight strap across the torso. His hair curls down his back and his robe is slipping sensuously down his hips, revealing the top of his buttocks. A man in a football shirt and checked knee-length shorts circles him hesitantly, then goes to a landscape on the wall. A cleaner briskly pushes her broom past.

The statue, by Jacob Epstein, stands in the centre of a circular foyer in Birmingham Museum and Art Gallery, with walls of Pompeian red hung with watercolours and oils. For four months in 2010 and 2011 a cloak of green silk carnations flowed from his hands and spilled luxuriously down the plinth to the floor. This 'intervention' was part of an exhibition, 'Queering the Museum', curated by ceramicist Matt Smith. It aimed to draw out LGBT (lesbian, gay, bisexual, transgender) themes from the museum's collection, or impose them on it. Green carnations were worn by men at the end of the 19th and early 20th century to signify homosexuality. Oscar Wilde wore one, and an 1894 novel written by Robert Hichens, *The Green Carnation*, contained characters based on Wilde and his lover Lord Alfred Douglas, friends of Hichens. The book was used by the prosecution in Wilde's trial for gross indecency in 1895.

Other objects from Birmingham's collection in the exhibition were a willow pattern drug jar which Smith linked with HIV, and 'Swiss Boy', a china figurine jauntily stepping along wearing a large floppy hat and knee-length breeches. Smith placed him with one of his own ceramic figures (wearing a green carnation at groin height) and renamed the boy 'Figure of a Youth Cruising'. Another exhibit was a statuette Smith made of the 'Ladies of Llangollen', Sarah Ponsonby and Eleanor Butler, who left their aristocratic Irish homes in 1778 and lived together for 51 years in Wales, united by 'something more tender still than friendship'.

The exhibition catalogue explained that 'the luxury of [the museum's] authoritative and contemplative space is always predicated upon exclusion' which may be 'intolerant of atypical narratives'. The exhibition is 'a deliberate act of wilful confusion and disorder, a rummaging through the museum dressing up box to see what we might be missing.'

Matt Smith spoke about Lucifer, about putting the exhibition together and why he thinks it important to make objects tell new stories.

> The museum that I first got emotionally involved with was Birmingham Museum & Art Gallery when I was an undergraduate in the city. One day I came across the label for a Simeon Solomon painting that mentioned same-sex relationships, which was really shocking for that time. This was 1991– Clause 28 was in, local authorities weren't allowed to promote homosexuality, AIDS was in its heyday. For Birmingham Museum to mention it quietly on a label seemed a huge thing. The label then went on to link same-sex attraction with ending up in a poorhouse – so it was like 'Wow, this is a great thing and it's not so great as well.' It was a very small thing that stayed with me and that I wanted to start playing with when I worked with the collections at Birmingham.
>
> When I started the 'Queering the Museum' project I looked up 'gay and lesbian' and 'LGBT' on the Birmingham objects database and nothing came up. When I looked up 'queer' one object came up, which was a Burne-Jones photogravure of a small child who was described as having a 'queer elfin beauty', which I love, but it shows how little in the museum was explicitly linked to LGBT lives.
>
> I knew the Lucifer sculpture; I must have been walking past it for years. When the Curator of Fine Art, Victoria Osborne, asked whether I had thought about working with

it, I asked why. It turns out that Epstein sculpted it with the body of a man and the face and head of a woman. As soon as you know that, it becomes a transgressive, trans-object. I was really fascinated that even when you are looking out for queer signals in a museum, they need to be pointed out to you.

I had a sense that I wanted to make it a signpost for the exhibition, but it was a real struggle working out how to do that with this huge bronze statue. We had lots of discussions – do we put a pair of Speedos on him? A rainbow flag? The only way I felt comfortable with working with the statue – for which I have great respect – was by draping it with thousands of artificial green carnations – a flower which Oscar Wilde used as a means of signifying his homosexuality to other men. There's something really satisfying about going into a fabric shop to measure up a cloak for an Epstein sculpture. I had a friend come over and the two of us sat with sewing machines and had a marathon sewing bee!

I think it was one of the most successful interventions because of its scale, although there was something odd about subverting someone else's work. There is a lot in Milton's *Paradise Lost* describing Lucifer as an angel trying to overthrow God and being exiled into Hell – so there was lots of play about mainstream and minority positions going on with Lucifer as a transgressive figure, which worked for the exhibition. I was interested in parallels with how society deals with people who don't conform. For me it raised a lot of readings.

Museums are really good on keywords and ways of describing objects, but until those keywords start to describe marginalised lives, every time anyone starts doing this type of work they're going to have to re-audit the collection. It feels like a real loss that this auditing is not put on a more permanent footing.

I don't think any museum or art gallery in England has completely cracked how best to reflect LGBT lifestyles, though I think things are getting better. Partly people tend not to think about it unless it affects them, but also sexuality and museums aren't very easy bedfellows. Museums deal with objects and there aren't that many that are intrinsically gay. If they are solely dealing with objects in terms of when they're made, who they're made by, what they made of, then it's going to be difficult. So I'd like to see museums moving away from the old-fashioned cataloguing way of describing objects and linking them much more to the lived lives of objects; but that's quite a change. Museums deal with things that are evidenced and written and a lot of stories marginalised groups tell are not documented well. I think oral histories have much more potential to bring out queer narratives.

With civil partnerships and now gay weddings suddenly there's a wealth of material culture coming out that can be linked to gay men and women in a way that it couldn't before. It's great that legal records to do with LGBT lives are no longer all criminal records.

Museums have a really weird dichotomy for me. As a gay man I never saw myself represented in them but at the same time they're quite charged spaces because people are walking around looking. There's something going on between the visitors and objects, and also the visitors looking at each other... and I like that tension. E.M. Forster references cruising in museums and Isaac Julien's directed films about it – it pops up now and again. Museum-going and the way gay men sometimes interact with each other both involve picking up on visual clues and signals. There are close parallels.

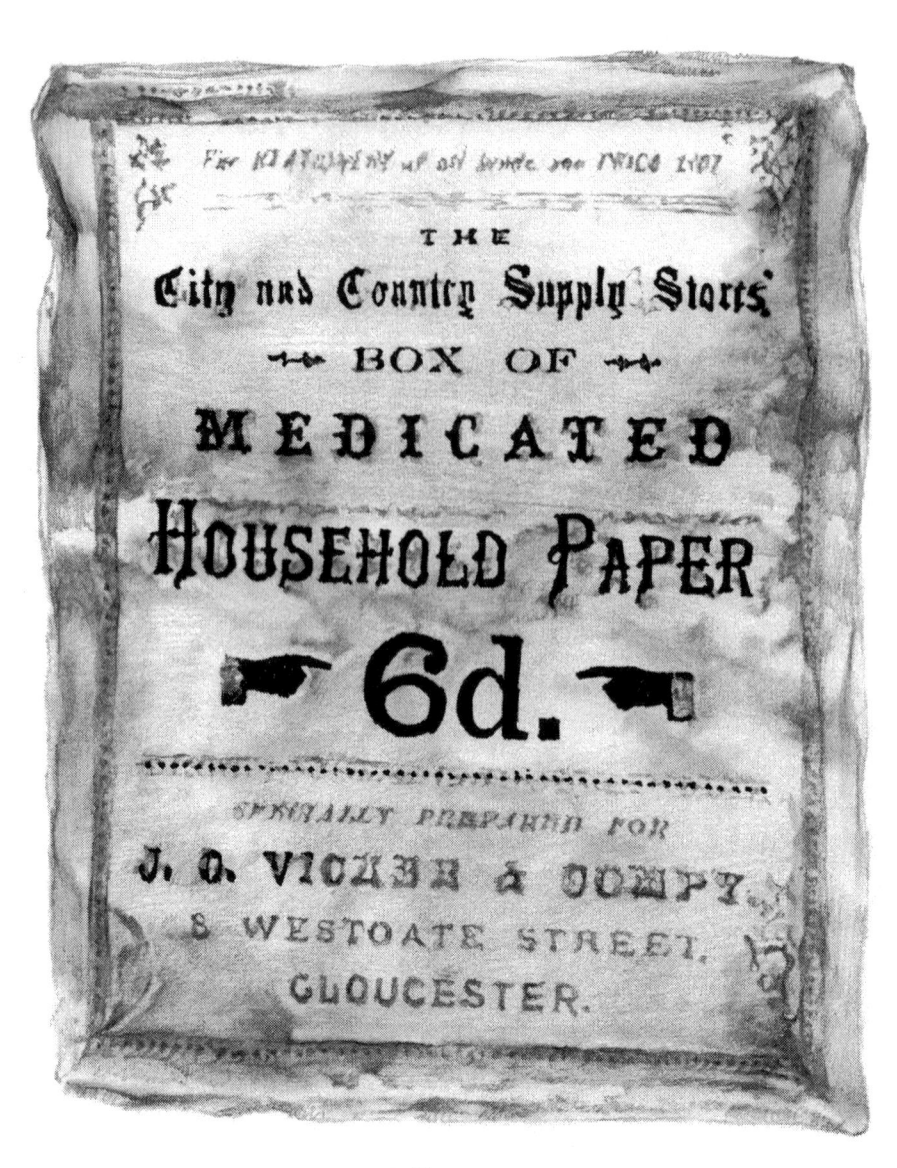

Toilet paper
Land of Lost Content

The Ephemeral

THE WORD 'EPHEMERAL' comes from the Greek for 'lasting only one day'. Collector Maurice Rickards, who helped to raise the status of ephemera in the UK, defined it as 'the minor transient documents of everyday life'. In his view leaflets, posters or coupons could evoke past times as vividly as legal writs or letters, and revealed parts of life which would otherwise go unrecorded. Anyone who has found that advertisements are as good as news bulletins at capturing the flavour and concerns of an era will agree. Such documents also record often ignored aspects of history – not momentous events or significant shifts in opinion or sensibility, but routines and habits.

Large collections of ephemera are usually made by individuals rather than institutions, but often end up in museums, which may be very grateful for a complete set of football programmes or theatre tickets. Sometimes they become archives in their own right. Robert Opie's collection of packaging, put together over 20 years, is now the Museum of Brands, Packaging and Advertising. Opie declares this collection is valuable evidence of 'a dynamic commercial system that delivers thousands of desirable items from all corners of the world, a feat arguably more complex than sending man to the Moon, but one still taken for granted.' Nor is ephemera collecting a purely recent phenomenon; Sarah Sophia Banks, sister of explorer Joseph Banks, collected coins, leaflets, tickets and newspaper cuttings in the late 18th and early 19th centuries, some of which records events for which there is no other evidence.

Gathering digital ephemera is an especially interesting area. Should text messages, e-mails and webpages be collected? If so, how? What about privacy laws and commercial concerns? The British Library has been archiving selected websites since 2004, and in April 2013 announced it wanted to expand this to include every page in the UK web domain. However, in practice this goal is still some way off, and legal considerations mean that this comprehensive archive can only be accessed from the library's physical site in London. Other organisations, such as the National Libraries of Spain and France, have similar aims for all webpages published in their countries.

Ephemera from three centuries appear in this section. The first object is a 19th-century leaflet advertising a live mermaid, introduced by the director of the Centre for Ephemera Studies at Reading University. The second, from the early 20th century, is a packet of toilet paper, perhaps the most transient product one could imagine. Its owner speaks of her love for it. The third is a page from a politician's Twitter feed, part of the British Library's UK web archive. Their Head of Archiving describes how the Library has tackled the particular challenges of maintaining digital collections.

MERMAID FLYER

*The Maurice Rickards collection,
Centre for Ephemera Studies, Reading University*

CATALOGUING EPHEMERA requires extra-long lists. Adverts, notices, coupons, business cards, labels. Tickets, forms, memos, stationery, menus. Maurice Rickards's 20,000-strong collection of these and other items forms the core collection at the Centre for Ephemera Studies in Reading University's Department of Typography & Graphic Communication. The categories of ephemera in the centre's collection has a marvellous randomness: Magic lantern, Map, Market, Market plan, Market prices, Marriage, Marrow bones, Matches, Maxim card, Mechanical, Medal, Medical, Menswear, Membership card.

One piece, kept in a folder under plastic, is a roughly A4-sized advertising leaflet with a black border. It declares:

> For a short time only. Just arrived in this town, the only real mermaid in the kingdom, caught ALIVE, off the Shetland Islands, by a fisherman.

It continues:

> This wonderful Nondescript is upwards of two feet in length, having very short arms, and webbed between the fingers. Her head is very long, thick curly hair, no ears, but nature has supplied her with gills like a fish. The lower part of the breast is covered with scales, and the tail and fins are very large and strong. She was taken in a storm on the 2nd of March last, and the only specimen that has been preserved in this country. Although many persons have seen such creatures, it is the link in nature that

connects the human being and the fish, the same as the monkey, bat, and seal connect the various species of the animal creation. This curiosity was exhibited before the College of Surgeons, Aberdeen, who declared it well worthy the inspection of the curious.

But in the top right-hand corner someone has written 'this bill was left at my house Friday 26 Oct 1849. Curiosity tempted me to give a penny to see ye "<u>Wonderful</u> <u>work</u> <u>of</u> <u>God</u>". But of all ye <u>impositions</u> which my eyes ever saw this bang'd them all!' Then there is a signature and a place: 'Piercebridge, near Darlington'.

The leaflet raises several intriguing questions. Robert Chambers's *Vestiges of the Natural History of Creation* had been published in 1844 (five years before the leaflet was delivered), popularising the idea of transmutation of species and of evolution. Are the leaflet's assertions about relationships between species ('the link in nature that connects the human being and the fish') a garbled version of ideas from *Vestiges*? Was there really any connection with the College of Surgeons at Aberdeen? What was actually being displayed – a child? A small woman? Who was the disillusioned author of the critical comment writing for?

Michael Twyman, director of the Centre for Ephemera Studies, explains why he thinks the flyer is important.

> This is a bill advertising a freak show of the mid-19th century. It is one of the most symbolic objects in the collection – it epitomises what ephemera are all about. It has a focus on the particular, which very few other kinds of documents do. It is evidence for delivery of publicity from house-to-house in the 19th century. The language of ephemera is very revealing – all kinds of terms crop up that we're not used to. 'Bang'd them all' – that's surely street language.

It was printed in a mixture of typefaces, with the words 'Real Mermaid' picked out in condensed fat-face letters, and has at its head a stock image of a ship to emphasize that the mermaid was caught by a fisherman. It has no imprint, which means that its printer was breaking the law.

The addition of personal comments (we don't know whether the writer is a man or woman) make it rather special. Mermaids were regularly illustrated in bestiaries, but did people really believe in them? Here is evidence that one person didn't. This is a carefully thought out response – certain words, such as 'imposition' are carefully underlined with a separate pen. Then the item got kept, which is even more extraordinary. This person wanted to leave something to posterity and say something about how his or her period would be judged. It's been done for the record and is an archivist's dream – it's dated.

I have half-jokingly suggested that 'ephemerology' should be an academic discipline – until you have a name for something no one takes it seriously. But the importance of ephemera is now recognized within the curatorial world. Such documents are relatively free of the baggage of other written forms and of canons of taste and judgement that have been passed down over the years. An item is of interest simply for what it tells you, and as a starting point that is valuable. As time passes there will be judgements made. We are only at the very beginning of taking ephemera seriously.

Toilet Paper

Land of Lost Content, Craven Arms

UP A SIDE STREET in the Shropshire town of Craven Arms stands the Land of Lost Content Museum in an imposing orange and yellow brick church-like building, actually the old market hall. Bunting, bright signs and miscellaneous objects are spread outside – a rocking horse, a vintage car. An open suitcase near the door turns out to hold a 'vitalitor', a decades-old handheld device for applying electricity to the body for health purposes. Next to it is a blacksmith's bellows.

Inside is a crazy world, as a prominent handwritten sign freely admits:

This museum is the work of two people – Stella and Dave Mitchell.
All removals, displays and building work.
No one else involved!
No grant funding!
No safety net!
No sense at all!
We both hope you enjoy it...

Next to it are a Bethel Baptist Sunday school banner, Beano annuals and a sad notice:

Gone – but not forgotten. Two Edwardian dolls were stolen from this display a few months into 2006. I have stopped crying for them in the night now, but I shall mourn till the day I die.

The museum's collection is jointly owned by Stella and by fashion designer Wayne Hemingway, who has used it as inspiration for household products and an online educational resource. The building is packed with things – clothes, kitchenware, sweets, records, board games, dolls holding dolls. The C5, Clive Sinclair's

1985 plastic electric vehicle is there, as are Subbuteo, Kidditunes ('Fun and joy for girl and boy') and an early mobile phone almost too heavy to lift – used mainly on building sites, the label says. Coronation Street fridge magnets jostle with chairlifts and government leaflets ('July 5, 1948 sees the fulfilment of that promise with the inauguration of the social security scheme – a great and human plan worthy of a proud people').

Mannequins stand in the half-light – one with a Lyons Maid ice cream tray, one dressed as a rockabilly next to a jukebox, another in a red and yellow sweatshirt from a clowns' convention. One, wearing carpet slippers, lies collapsed in an armchair under a 1969 copy of the Chichester Observer, perhaps overwhelmed by the stuff around him. Costumes from the 2012 Olympic Opening Ceremony (acquired via Oxfam) are hanging on the front door. Crooning music provides a melancholy accompaniment as one strolls around – 'Begin the Beguine', 'If I Had My Way'.

Handwritten signs on fluorescent card give Stella Mitchell's views. One by a school display says:

> *A child in a liberty bodice, vest, Viyella blouse and woollen cardigan felt cosy, warm and protected. That's what's wrong with children today – too much LIBERTY, not enough BODICE.*

Another, by a 'table tales' display proclaims:

> *Everyone began to need more time in the 60s – too much to do, too much TV to watch. Enter the instant food. Style-wise there was Habitat and Scandinavian wood. Lots of orange and lots of big flowers.*

This last sign highlights something which puzzles me while walking around – the fact that the museum seems to both criticise and celebrate a throwaway culture. It mourns the lifestyle changes which are caused by, and demand, a constant supply of new consumer goods. But it cherishes these goods too.

I ask Stella to pick one object to talk about. She fetches a square packet of toilet paper, the size of a small notebook, labelled 'Medicated Household Paper, 6d'.

> A recent acquisition, this was brought in by a local lady who found it on a tip. I have many different toilet rolls, hard and soft (the first soft toilet tissue came out in this country in 1947). This is the earliest one I've ever seen and I'm so pleased to get it.
>
> It's made of individual sheets. You couldn't get it from chemists; it was sold by stationers. It wasn't as thin as later and it hasn't got the gloss side and the matt side.
>
> It cost sixpence, so I'm imagining it is from the early to mid-1920s. At that time sixpence was a heck of a lot of money and only very rich people bothered with this stuff at all. Until the 1950s most people used cut-up newspaper, second-hand paper of all sorts.
>
> I've got a toilet roll in my collection called 'Everest – the peak of toilet tissue' with a picture of Mount Everest on the wrapper. You never have to pay that much to collect toilet paper, it's usually about £3.50 per roll, or a good one like the Everest you might pay at the most £7 or £8 for, even now.
>
> There is always something new. So I look round the supermarket for a new toilet roll wrapper. And it all makes a kind of sense to me and to anyone who is interested in the scheme of social history. Who changes life the most? People who invented soft toilet tissue have made our lives so much easier.
>
> I'm mostly interested in ordinary people's lives rather than the lives of the wealthy. Other museums have always

bothered with things that were made for rich people – vases, gorgeous statues, wall tapestries. I wouldn't go to a stately home if it was on my doorstep – I'm not remotely interested in how the rich have lived in the past, it's not real.

So don't come here looking for Dior dresses – but you will see old vests. I've got a fabulous vest, and it's got darning on the backside – a person has handknitted this vest, it's the tiniest little stitches you ever saw, and the lady has had to maintain her vest – it's darn on top of darn, and to me that's a wonderful piece of costume.

My friends think I'm barking mad, especially as I've already got enough in the museum; why do I spend every spare minute going out into the world to find more? It's because I am a collector, not a museum owner. I walk across the road to the charity shop three times a day and come back with something each time, so all the time this collection is getting bigger and more unwieldy and harder to maintain. But I can't help it because there are things out there that need to be looked after and put with others of their ilk, and toilet rolls don't say much about anything, but you put it in the stream of history, immediately you're going – oh! – that really tells you something about how things have changed.

There are 14 storerooms in the building, packed to the gunwales. When I acquire something I'll look after it, I'll clean it, I accept things into the family like a love process I go through. Everything here I know.

The first thing I ever collected were some Edwardian carte de visite photos. I was seven or eight years old – this was in the 1950s, and at that time such things had no value. There were 15 to 20 people in the photos, stiff ladies and gentlemen in outrageous kit, awful black and grey suits up to their earholes. And yet they walked outside in the sunshine as I did. I found myself asking questions about them – who they were, what they did. It was a shame those people had to disappear, and I kept the cards.

I was always a questioner. I don't think you ever answer the questions, but I know a lot about different periods of time now. For example, Edwardian people wore heavy underwear to keep them warm and stop smells emerging. They had linen buttons since they had to boil the clothes. So I've learned those sorts of reasons for the clothes.

The museum is called the Land of Lost Content because in the poem A E Housman is talking about the past being a country to which you cannot return, though you can look at it. I like to make people think about the poem, so it's on the wall in the ladies' toilet, it's on the blackboard in school display. The museum is also about respect for objects. Things are too easily available now. Until we ban imports from China we're on a hiding to nothing, using and chucking.

I'm happy if people think it's spooky – I try hard –for example by using low lights. People are occasionally freaked by the mannequins though, and even have to go out and sit down.

I'm aware that the idea or ambience of the museum could be thought a little bit on the maudlin side of things. How would you do it otherwise? Bright lights and clean plastic, making it all look dirty? It wouldn't work. You don't want to do that with old things – you want to put them on an old shelf. A lot of our shelf units are got from skips and tips. I'm a fine artist, it's got to look right. And if it looks a bit like a mausoleum – good. It makes people think. We're only here for a short time, as are the things we leave behind us.

Stella also mentions that she regularly gets calls from Museum Studies students doing research, and I am not surprised. The museum lends itself to fascinating interpretations. A critique of consumer culture. A museum taken to its logical extreme – if we were really to document and understand the past through objects, it might take something like this. A rejection of the idea that collecting can ever be rationalised with mission statements, cataloguing procedures and conservation policies. Evidence that objects must be disposed of and forgotten or they will overwhelm us.

In the end though, my strongest impression is of a woman who loves objects and loves what they tell us about life. In his book *The Comfort of Things*, Daniel Miller investigates the meaning of objects to people in one London street, and concludes that people who have close relationships with objects usually have close relationships with people. I mention this to Stella, and she agrees.

JONATHAN FRYER'S TWITTER FEED

The British Library, London

'TIME FOR LORD ASHCROFT TO FESS UP,' says the July 2009 Twitter feed of Jonathan Fryer, Liberal Democrat candidate in the 2014 European elections. Fryer is a journalist and writer, and lectures at London universities as well as giving British Council and government-sponsored lectures abroad on democracy-building and the media. Other tweets on the same page say: 'Heading for the Sutton LibDem annual garden party, hoping the sun breaks through and Charles Kennedy turns up'; 'Went to see *Bruno*; a real curate's egg, but two or three brilliant scenes'; and 'Just purged 8 American floozies from my followers. How do they get to latch onto one like limpets?' What strikes me as I read the feed now, is how much goes on in our lives concurrently that we later forget – plays and politics, weather and admin.

This Twitter page is in the British Library's UK Web archive, in a section where curators have selected websites likely to be of long-term interest. This part of the archive is available to anyone with an internet connection, and people can nominate sites for inclusion. Also chosen are sites about the 2012 Olympics and Paralympics, the 2005 London terrorist attacks, Quakers, and the Queen's Diamond Jubilee. Some capture immediate reactions. The 'Europhobia' site for July 7 2005, the day of the London terrorist attacks, starts with: 'So, what's this "bang" on the tube all about then? Anyone got any clearer idea than "either a bomb or a big crash"? And does this count as Sod's Law, coming the day after the Olympics announcement?'

Two pages from Fryer's Twitter feed are in a section devoted to blogs, containing 756 sites. It rubs shoulders with 'Jazz Cat' (bass guitarist Ben Crosland) and 'JonnyB's Private Secret Diary' (Norfolk Village Life: Exposed). All these are still going in 2015, the latter with a book based on the blog, *Sex and Bowls and Rock 'n' Roll*. But the bulk archiving of Twitter, at least, must be less valuable for individual pages than for tracking how opinions – those expressed online, anyway – spread and change en masse.

Helen Hockx-Yu, Head of Archiving, explained why the library archives Twitter pages.

> Under the 2003 legal deposit regulations, the British Library is obliged to collect the intellectual output of this country, and this includes digital publications. Before 2013, we collected websites selectively, prioritising websites which reflect the diversity of life in the UK, those which are

about national events of social or economic interest, those which are likely to be of research interest, and lastly websites which show web innovation. But now we are collecting everything with a .uk domain name, or webpages with other domain names where the publishing process takes place wholly or partly in the UK.

I'm not worried about information overload – we miss so much! Ten million UK domain name registrations last December – and it's growing by 13% -17% each year, and that's just registration. We're only archiving once a year, so no, we won't be able to get everything. It's like a snapshot.

We are not systematically archiving Twitter – it's not technically easy, and it's not clear if it's published in the UK or not. If it comes to an important event such as the death of Margaret Thatcher or of Nelson Mandela curators can select and we will archive Twitter pages of people or organisations who have played a part in that person's life.

One of the things we've done with Jonathan Fryer's Twitter page is ensure its existence. The other thing we've done is place it into a wider context, along with websites on a similar theme. It's not very different from how libraries traditionally organise collections and knowledge. But there are things you can't capture. For example, what about the people that followed this person and commented on them?

The fact that something is ephemeral actually increases its significance sometimes. For example, we have the only copy of the website of the late politician Robin Cook. Another example is Antony Gormley's 2009 art project One and Other in which 2000 people stood up on the fourth plinth in Trafalgar Square and made a statement. This was videoed and streamed, and we have that website in the archives.

Web page creators may request for a page to be taken down from the archive, and they will be in cases such as breaches of confidentiality or defamation. But more generally, people who put things on the web thinking this is just a harmless personal rant or whatever, need to think about it. There are search engines using robots to crawl and index the web. Even if you take the page down you might leave traces which you may regret. So if you're not sure, don't do it!

We now see webpages as data to be analysed rather than in a more traditional way as documents. Now we are working with scholars to think about the patterns and trends which people may be interested in finding. For example, we could analyse how websites are linked together – which government departments' websites are linked to others, say.

There are interesting things you can discover. For example there is a Tibetan fruit called a goji berry which is seen as a superfood. If you go to the web archive and use the N-gram search, which visualises a full-text search, you can see that this started to become popular in the UK around 2007, followed by an increasing presence on the web. Doing this kind of analysis allows you to discover when something started to appear or became important.

Jonathan Fryer told me what value he thought his Twitter feed had now.

I think it's a good idea to archive Twitter feeds. In a sense, Twitter has taken over from letters and other forms of exchange of information and ideas. I'm a writer of biographies and to research a biography you have to rely on letters, diaries and other things which have been left behind. But that sort of source material is very rare these days, so forms of communication such as blogs and Twitter need to be kept instead. Also, evidence of the nature of the Twitter phenomenon itself is valuable.

A lot of Twitter is ephemeral and perhaps not worth keeping, but more important subjects do come up, and comments on them do resonate later. For example, domestic political developments or events abroad such as the war in Syria. These are often complex stories and people's responses on Twitter are evidence of that. I first started using it because of the Egyptian revolution – it was the best way of finding out what was going on.

My archived Twitter page is a mixed bag. The visit to the Sutton LibDem garden party is of no permanent interest, but other things are – the fact that it picked up on things that have turned into scandals – phone hacking, the Ashcroft business. I follow writers on Twitter, who often use it to push their books and try to shape opinions since very few newspapers carry book reviews now, and people don't want to read long book reviews anyway.

I suppose my feed is interesting to me personally to find out what I was thinking about and doing in the past. I used to keep a diary, but now I blog and tweet instead.

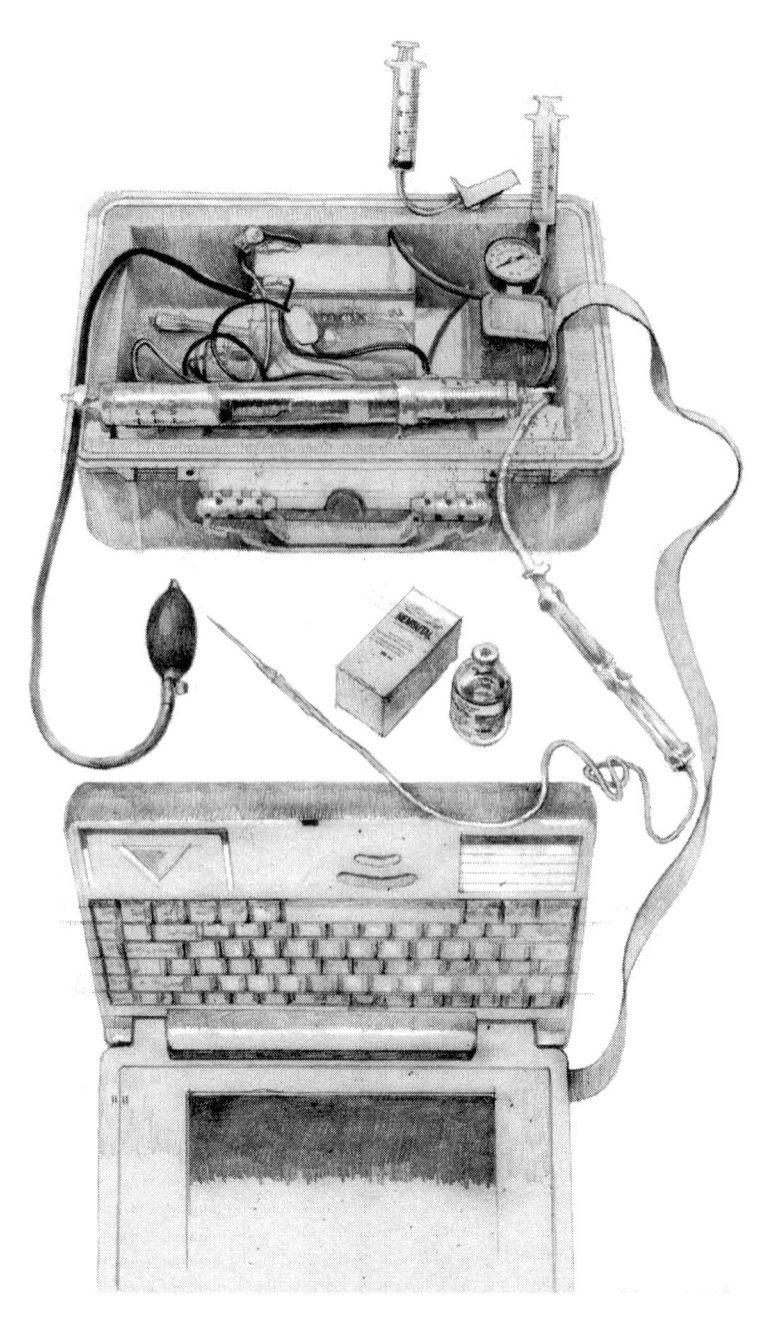

Euthanasia machine
Science Museum

The Lethal

CAN A LETHAL OBJECT BE ATTRACTIVE? How should museums present and interpret objects which kill? The proprietor of the Museum of Death in Hollywood, JD Healy, speaks approvingly of the 'falling-down ovation' the objects in his museum receive when visitors faint. His museum holds a speeding ticket James Dean received shortly before his fatal car crash, and the head of a French serial killer guillotined in 1922. He claims that the museum's main aim is to provoke thought about death, but there is no doubt that it exploits the exhibits' macabre associations for effect, displaying footage of people dying, and boasting of its 'replicas of full-size execution devices, mortician and autopsy instruments, pet death taxidermy, and so much more!' Most museums will want to avoid striking this sensationalist note, but may themselves have stuffed pets and even real execution devices to show.

The three things in this section kill for different reasons, and the death they bring can be accidental or intentional, welcome or unwelcome. The first is the element mercury, with which society has a precarious relationship. Over centuries scientists, designers and entrepreneurs have tried to release its beauty and maximise its utility and at the same time understand its deadly effects. Campaigning pressure and government regulations are an essential part of protecting us from it. We meet it here in three everyday products. One of these, skin lightening cream, is still sold even though it contains levels of mercury banned by many governments.

The second two objects are man-made machines which kill. The first is a beautifully crafted 200-year-old gun. Gallery staff think this has been fired, but it is primarily a luxury gift unlikely to have been used on anyone. The other is a euthanasia machine, anything but ornamental, which four people have used to end their lives. Unlike the gun, this caused protests when it was put on display, and still does.

Mercury

Ulster Museum, Belfast

'How magical a liquid metal must have seemed, when no framework existed to understand it or place it in context!' exclaims Theodore Gray in his book *The Elements*. 'Oh piffle,' he continues, 'mercury is every bit as magical today, no matter how much you know about it.'

In fact, mercury was long understood through a mythological framework, and to some extent still is, since it is named after the speedy Roman god of messengers and trade. Its chemical symbol, Hg, comes from *hydrargyrum*, a Latinized form of a Greek word meaning 'water-silver', since it flows and looks like silver; the same reason for its other name, 'quicksilver' ('quick' meaning 'living'). It owes its magic to an unusually low freezing point of − 38.83°C, making it the only metallic element which is liquid at room temperature.

Many of us have mercury in our teeth, or remember it in thermometers poked uncomfortably under our tongues. We have an uneasy *modus vivendi* with an element which is both poisonous and useful, and its uses are always open to reassessment (mercury thermometers, for example, are now being phased out for safety and environmental reasons although the three grams of mercury in them is unlikely to cause problems if it gets out).

'The Elements' exhibition at Ulster Museum was inspired by Theodore Gray's book. Its curator, Mike Simms, chose to place mercury in 'Elements of Death'. He explained why and talked about the three everyday products in the exhibition containing Hg – a hat, a mirror and a jar of skin cream.

> You can't do the exhibition the way Theodore Gray has in the book, starting with hydrogen at 1 and making your way through. Most visitors would be almost immediately lost

since it's not necessarily relevant to their lives. So there are themes – Elements of the Universe; Elements of the Earth, Elements of Life. The exhibition has gaps because some of the elements are hardly used at all. Some of the rare earths didn't get much of a mention. And then Elements of Death, things people are going to be familiar with – mercury, lead, arsenic, cadmium.

I'm trying to make the exhibition accessible by first of all including familiar objects, then new or amazing ones where people will say 'what the heck is that?' I wanted top hats because people are familiar with the Mad Hatter story from *Alice in Wonderland*. Mercury was used in the felting process, to stiffen the felt. There is a perhaps apocryphal story that this property of mercury was discovered by accident. One of the processes of making felt stiffen involves human urine (it was a pretty unpleasant job anyway). A hat worker in France noticed urine from one person produced felt that was much better than any other, because that person was being treated for syphilis with mercuric nitrate. So they started to use mercuric nitrate in hat making, and that led to the phrase 'mad as a hatter', because of the nerve damage it caused. They were still using mercury in felt stiffening in the 1960s.

For centuries mirrors were made using a mercury-silver amalgam. Because silver is the most reflective metal it could effectively create silver paint, which you put behind the sheet of glass to give you a brilliant surface. Over the decades the silver would crystallise out, so you get a lovely sparkly effect. The mercury also slowly moved downwards and the bottom part will have more mercury and will give off mercury vapour, but at levels too low to cause significant harm.

The exhibition also has a jar of Stillman's Skin Bleach Cream. There was a survey done by the Chicago Tribune in 2010 which tested 50 different skin lightening products used mainly by the Asian community. Five of these products were found to have mercury levels 1000 times above the limit. This brand contains the highest concentration by a long way – 3%. That's a high level. Skincare products containing mercury are banned across the USA, Canada, Europe – but this is still manufactured in Pakistan, by a company registered in the USA. I got a jar of this stuff on eBay from a chap in Manchester.

From coming across the book and putting together the exhibition was three and a half years. You have a picture in your mind of things you'd like to include and then there are the things that the museum actually has. And they do not necessarily match. Then it's a case of cutting your cloth – what do we have, what can we adapt, what are the things we can then buy to augment that. I spent quite a lot of time rummaging through the collections across the museum. I was really happy to find the mirror, but we don't know a lot about it. It was donated around 1910.

In the last 20 years or so, there's been a real clampdown on elements that are dangerous. Lead, for example, has been removed from nearly everything. But these elements are often incredibly useful. Electricians curse the day lead was removed from solder – it's strong and flexible.

By not using mercury we are missing out on a lot of fun because mercury is fantastic stuff to play with. It's really really dense, it goes into beads as you move it around, and you can float a cannonball on it. It's rather a shame that it's quite nasty.

FLINTLOCK PISTOLS

Kelvingrove Art Gallery and Museum, Glasgow

UP ON THE FIRST FLOOR of Kelvingrove Art Gallery and Museum, Robert Lyons Scott looks out from his portrait. He is sitting down, suited, a cigarette in his hand and his dog Scapegoat at his feet. Shadowy suits of armour glisten in the background. Lyons Scott was chairman of the Scotts' Shipbuilding and Engineering Company Ltd, the oldest ship building company in Britain and also a keen fencer, hunter and arms and armour collector.

Among his gifts to the city were a pair of presentation pistols made by Nicolas-Noël Boutet of Versailles in about 1802-10, now displayed in a gallery devoted to a history of Glasgow. The room contains arresting and challenging contrasts; there are also painter Ken Currie's vivid tableaux illustrating and inciting the class struggle. Workers' faces are picked out in lurid red and yellow against claustrophobic black backgrounds as they work and march and meet. They are in constricted, urgent, intense situations which do not admit the wider perspective which daylight would afford. We are told about 'the Scottish Lenin' John Maclean, who in the early 20th century campaigned against the exploitative working conditions which came with the transformation of Glasgow into the second city of the British Empire through its mining, shipbuilding and engineering industries.

The pistols share a display case with other gifts to the museum, and sit alongside an oak carving of St Catherine of Alexandria from about 1500 and a frog sculpture by French artist Niki de St Phalle.

Ralph Moffat, curator of European Arms and Armour, introduced the pistols, explained how they worked and talked about the best ways of displaying weapons.

> These pistols belonged to Robert Lyons Scott, a Greenock shipbuilder who was obsessed with arms and armour. He

bought his first pair of pistols when he was a young boy and collected them through his life, and on his death in 1939 he bequeathed his amazing collection to the people of Glasgow, who'd worked in his shipyards. He was a keen fencer, a great shot, a great hunter. He has the oldest near-complete plate armour in existence.

They are armes de luxe – the high end of arms and armour. Nicolas-Noël Boutet was one of the finest gun craftsmen in France and directed the Royal gun-making factory (renamed Imperial gunmakers after the revolution). Boutet is quite a sad character – he died in poverty after payments from the Imperial Arsenal ceased after Napoleon's death.

These are gifts, often to generals or to people who have achieved something in battle, or as part of diplomacy. It's about saying 'this is the best that France can offer'. The gold and silver might also remind the owner of trophies. This goes back to ancient Roman and Greeks who would take the weapons of defeated people and present them to the gods. They are working pistols, but someone of that rank would have a bodyguard as well – using the pistol would be very much a last resort.

The barrels have been blued – that's heat-treated, to change the colour, and that picks up the gold inlay. There's a beautiful Medusa's head chiselled on the butt cap. One of the gallery assistants here who's a keen shot with the replicas has said, from looking at the steel on the pan, that it's been fired several times, or at least the ignition has been used.

To fire the gun, first of all you check the barrel is clear and clean. You put your main powder in the barrel, and your priming powder in the pan (that's where you get the term flash in the pan–when the powder in the pan goes off but the main charge doesn't). Make sure the ball and wadding are tightly packed so that gases can build up. The cock is brought back and the mainspring is compressed. The trigger is pulled, it releases the cock and strikes off the steel, often called the flint. The spark lights the priming powder – (there's a touch hole which must be kept clear with the touch hole pricker), which ignites and goes through to the main charge. That's when you get the slight delay between the flash and the shot itself. It's complicated but it works and is very reliable.

So along with the gun there are jams for clearing out the barrels, a ramrod for loading the pistol, a little screw called a worm which is used to pack wadding in with your bullet. There is often a bullet mould as well because the bullet has to fit the barrel just right.

Arms and armour is part of a world which is very alien to a lot of people, especially in an industrial society where everything is mass-produced. I want to draw people into that world, trying to get people to understand how such complex shapes can be made using metal tools like hammers and anvils. I've always been fascinated by arms and armour–as a child I used to visit castles and my dad would tell me stories of the Border Reivers and suchlike. At heart I'm very much a mediaevalist – I start to lose interest as you get into mass-produced things.

Armour is just pieces of metal, yes, but it is also a visceral link to that time. It's using the best technology to protect the body and take the lives of others, which of course people continue to do today. Someone sweated into that suit of armour. I'd ideally like to display the suits by shining red lights on them to evoke sweat and blood.

We don't get a lot of complaints about displaying weapons; story displays are about understanding the objects in the context. With something like a sword, which is a very skilfully designed tool for cutting off arms and severing arteries, that's what it's for; you can't fully understand something if you try and avoid that altogether. It's a case of treading carefully. Give people the information and they can make up their own minds.

EUTHANASIA MACHINE

Science Museum, London

THE EUTHANASIA MACHINE looks like an old-fashioned laptop connected to a set of gadgets and wires in an open plastic suitcase, with syringes and a gauge prominent. A white and yellow box of the barbiturate Nembutal stands in front of it. It has an unassuming position near a lift in the museum's Wellcome wing, part of an exhibition about controversial issues in science. Nearby is an artwork using scans of living human foetuses to question perceptions of disability. Another exhibit is a motor racing car in pieces after a crash from which the driver walked away unhurt, perhaps meant to provoke thought about the way in which technology encourages risk.

The machine uses software which asks the patient three questions, and automatically administers a lethal injection if the answer is 'yes' to each one. 'Are you certain you understand that if you proceed and press the 'yes' button on the next screen that you will die?' is the second question, which surely needs simplifying. However, the machine is not likely to be used again.

The machine was developed by Dr Philip Nitschke, a former doctor who founded Exit International, Australia's best-known pro-euthanasia organisation. Four people used it to end their lives between 1995 and 1997 in Australia's Northern Territory, when euthanasia was legal there. Nitschke then donated the machine to the museum, and it went on display in 2000.

In a 2002 interview with Australian magazine *Quadrant* Nitschke said that doctors should give patients information about assisted dying if they wanted it: 'It seems to me you lose the respect of society when a patient is in dire circumstances, and asks you what you can do to help, and you draw back and say, "I'm sorry, that is forbidden".' Describing the machine, he said: 'It was an arrangement by which a patient pressed a computer key three times, with a pause each time to reconsider his or her decision to die... I thought the patient should control the option to die. Also, I was not a family member. I was not a best friend. I did not want to occupy personal space that belonged to others.'

The museum has been careful to present the machine objectively; for example, the software is called 'Deliverance' and the equipment is sometimes called a 'deliverance machine' (for example, on Wikipedia) but the label does not use that term. Nevertheless, the decision to display it has aroused strong emotions and opinions. 'Upon recovering from my original shock, I...found it slightly offensive that they would put a tool for suicide on display at a museum that is frequented by families and schoolchildren,' wrote a blogger for the Susan B. Anthony List, an American anti-abortion organisation. The museum hosted a debate when it was put on display, and hopes it will continue to provoke thought.

Philip Nitschke described why he gave the machine to the museum and said how he hoped it would affect visitors.

> I'm very pleased the machine is still on display. When the euthanasia law in the Northern Territory of Australia was

overturned in March 1997 the machine had no further use and was acquired by Australia's largest science museum, the Powerhouse Museum in Sydney. But there was such an outcry, some from politicians, and one memorable statement in the house from a senator of the day that 'he didn't want the children of the nation being traumatised by that obscenity!'

Then the museum became nervous saying that if they took it, it could not go on display 'for a while'. On pressing them I found that they thought it might be in the basement for a decade. So I reneged on my offer to give it to them, and it was at that point that the British Science Museum (who had been watching events) made contact and said they wanted it. Even then, there were moves to prevent its export. So I was glad to get it out of the country and to London, and very glad to see the display when finished.

What the machine does is invite people to think about 'death', their death, the idea of controlling one's own death, and the future of technology in that role. The issue of euthanasia has become one of the cutting edge social issues of the decade in many Western nations, and Deliverance (along with Kevorkian's 'Mercitron' and 'Thanatron') are icons of this issue - and something I'm quite proud to have been associated with.

Incidentally, a sister machine was built for the opening of the new Museum of Old and New Art in Hobart, Tasmania, as part of an installation called 'My beautiful chair' in collaboration with sculptor Greg Taylor. Here people would sit down and operate the machine and press the 'yes' or 'no' keys, something which seemed to have a profound effect on many.

Andrew Lilley, a microbiologist at King's College London, has looked at the machine on several occasions. He talked about how it had influenced his thoughts:

> When I first saw the euthanasia machine, it was a really strong experience. I knew about euthanasia, I'd thought about it a bit, but seeing the reality completely changed how I felt about it. It made it real, immediate, not coming out of history.
>
> You knew that four people had died using it, and the ordinariness of the equipment compared with what they actually did with it is really quite shocking. I still in essence feel that people who want to end their lives should be able to, but I now understand better the caution some people have. And the piece of equipment helped me focus that. Those were actually the tubes down which the barbiturates passed that killed those four people and you think 'this is really it'.
>
> There are people who say 'let's simply change the law, let people decide'. I'm not saying those people are glib or unthinking; they've often been through very hard things. But it's a problem of getting somewhere by having two opposites. To be firmly pro-euthanasia is a very peculiar thing to be, and it would be flippant to be in favour of it and not actually almost at the point where you couldn't be in favour because of all the negatives.
>
> Why the individual object should be so significant, rather than watching films about it, reading about it, learning about it, is rather hard to put your finger on. I was wondering what else I had seen that was like that, and funnily enough also in the Science Museum a while ago they had the crystals from which the DNA structure was

first identified through crystallography by Franklin and Wilkins. Anyone can show you crystallised DNA, but that was the actual sample from which she'd picked her crystals and put them in the machine. That only means something to you if you already have an engagement with the history of DNA and you did it as an undergraduate and it's been part of your life, but because it was the original sample and you have an idea about the sort of chemistry that was involved, it was special.

I've been seeing the euthanasia machine for a long time, and in that time the public discussion of it has moved on. Also I've been to quite a few funerals, including one person who had a form of euthanasia. I'm glad that I had the experience of seeing the machine early because it helped me to think about the reality rather than the theory. I sometimes pass by it again to see if that impact is still alive. And it is – obviously not as sharp as when I first saw it, but I'm glad it's still there.

Crocodile handbag
Cole Museum of Zoology

The Dead

PERHAPS ALL MUSEUM OBJECTS ARE DEAD. After all, they have been removed from everyday life, taken out of the places where they were used or loved. They are also given a kind of immortality, kept for decades or centuries, carefully prevented from ageing. The similarity between the words 'museum' and 'mausoleum', or burial chamber, has often been noticed. The 19th century French literary critic and art collector Edmond De Goncourt compared museums to tombs, and ordered that his Far Eastern art collection be auctioned off rather than displayed in a gallery, writing: 'My wish is that my drawings, prints, bibelots and books – the works of art which have been the joy of my life – should not be consigned to the cold tomb of a museum and the uncultivated glance of the indifferent passerby.'

The exhibits in this section died in different ways – one under the wheels of a car or motorbike, one probably hunted, one of natural causes. The first is an owl, the second a crocodile, the third a human being – the philosopher Jeremy Bentham, a man who campaigned for dead bodies to serve the living by being used for medical purposes before being buried. But he also asked that his own body be preserved and displayed in perpetuity, and his wishes were fulfilled. Visitors to

University College London can now decide whether he is in a 'cold tomb' or if his memory or even his ideas are in some sense kept alive through the display of his skeleton.

BARN OWL

Booth Museum of Natural History, Brighton

THE BOOTH MUSEUM stands on a main road in Hove, west of Brighton, facing public gardens and the sea shimmering beyond. Founded by naturalist and collector Edward Booth, it opened in 1891, stocked with over 300 cases containing stuffed birds in recreations of their natural surroundings. Booth, who shot birds and aimed to collect one of every British variety, was a pioneer of these 'diorama' settings. Over time the Booth added specimens of mammals, insects, minerals, and plants to its collection and became a museum of natural history in 1971.

Bird dioramas cover the walls from floor to ceiling. A red-necked grebe dives among reeds, a barred warbler stands on the edge of its nest in the tree trunk, parrot crossbills pluck at a bush. An imitation Victorian study at the centre of the museum recreates this collecting world with a desk covered in red cloth, magnifying glasses, and tiny drawers for specimens.

The museum is still collecting and stuffing birds, but not shooting them. Jeremy Adams, retired assistant keeper of natural sciences at the Booth, describes stuffing one of the birds on display, a barn owl, and explains how the museum acquires birds now.

This barn owl is one which I stuffed – taxidermied, if you want to be polite – about 15 years ago. It was brought into me as a road casualty, like most things that come into this museum. Of course I've always rather laughed at the idea of a car being a form of natural mortality, but I suppose it is, by today's standards. Anyway, it's very efficient, far more efficient than a hundred Mr Booths.

The ideal time to deal with the creature is directly after it's dead. And a poor second is to freeze it, which is what we inevitably have to do since we can't deal with the specimen straightaway. So they go into the freezer – a sort of taxidermy larder – after which they come out when their number comes up. Then we have to leave them to defrost (I experimented with microwaves but it was never satisfactory). And then the specimen is skinned, the skin cleaned, preserved and degreased, along with the bits of the skeleton you want to keep attached to it. And then they are washed, rinsed and blow-dried. A lot of taxidermy birds take some teasing and primping with their feathers. And then you make an artificial body. In my case the artificial body is made of wood wool – a shredded softwood. You wrap it in a cunning way with strong string to achieve an irregular shape – it's a form of sculpting. And you then stitch the artificial body into the skin, incorporating support wires, and position the bird and feathers exactly as you want them, choose and insert the correct eyes, and let it dry out. I try to achieve a realistic and lifelike specimen. Without being sentimental, I would want to do my best by them.

You can hide certain imperfections – in Mr Booth's day, he'd make sure the bullet holes didn't show. There's quite often a worst side – Victorian taxidermists would often arrange the set so that the best side showed.

When Mr Booth did his work here, taxidermy was cutting-edge technology. And the growing army of urban people would have no chance at all of seeing in the wild the dozens and dozens of creatures that he brought in here. Looking at a stuffed animal is not a substitute for watching a real bird but it definitely has its place. They don't bite you, they don't make a mess, and they keep still. For artists or sculptors who want to reproduce something, to be able to look at it from all different angles is unusual – you can't peep under the tail or under the chin of a real animal.

Owls are particularly popular – owls and frogs, it's curious. I think it's something to do with forward facing eyes – they're slightly more anthropomorphic. Barn owls are very beautiful birds, with their big facial discs.

CROCODILE HANDBAG

Cole Museum of Zoology, Reading

THE COLE is in Reading University's Zoology Department, an anonymous building tucked away on the campus. Inside you are greeted by the skeletons of an elephant (which came from a circus; blue-green shackle marks remain on its tusks), a false killer whale (a member of the dolphin family which looks like a whale), and a python. Giant spider crab skeletons are bright on a blue background on a far wall, and a turtle shell is suspended on a pillar. Pickled animals in jars – sponges, corals, frogs and many more – are in display cases, with labels trying to breathe life into them by explaining their habits and habitats.

Visitors can peer through windows to see the zoology lab next door, with rows of microscopes and more pickled animals on shelves. The museum holds human embryos, prepared so that the skeletons can be seen, to demonstrate how bones develop from cartilage as the foetus grows. These are not displayed for fear of upsetting people.

The crocodile handbag is in a display on man's impact on the environment. The animal's skin has been cut along its underside, opened out and flattened, so that its front legs, which would have been underneath its body, are on the front flap of the bag alongside its head, which has a blank stare and a forced grin. These legs have been doubled over to make decorative stubs. The knobbly texture of the animal's back forms a panel on the bag, and the skin on top of its head has been formed into a square shape to match. Tasselled plaits made of its skin lie next to its head.

Cole Museum curator and Zoology lecturer Amanda Callaghan describes how the handbag came to be in the collection, and why the museum displays it.

> This handbag was confiscated at Heathrow Airport. It would have been from someone who went on holiday and for some reason thought that it would be a nice handbag to have, which I really can't imagine because I think it's really hideous. People I suppose want something like this because they think it's funny or curious, but if they're caught it will be confiscated.
>
> The UK Border Agency has a list of items confiscated at Heathrow – wolf pelts and snakeskins, for example. Museums can register to go onto a rota, and you wait until

you get to the top. They send you a list of items and you can claim them for your museum, on permanent loan. I'd been waiting for a long time to get to the top of the list. The reason they give them to places like the Cole Museum is for education. I think it is important to highlight issues around the exploitation of endangered species so that people think twice before supporting the industry.

People have said why don't we burn it? What's the difference between you importing it and getting it from Heathrow? I think there is a massive difference because we wouldn't have supported the killing of animals for their skins.

I first heard about this system at the Rutland Bird Fair. They had wildlife police there and they had an enormous stuffed lion. I went up to one of the policeman and asked where he had acquired it. He gave me contact details for the UK Border Agency. But I suspect the lions go to the big museums.

JEREMY BENTHAM'S AUTO-ICON

University College London

THE CLOTHED SKELETON of one of the most influential figures in English philosophy and law sits in a polished mahogany box in a corner of a busy corridor in University College London (UCL). His glasses and pipe are on a table next to him, and his walking stick rests against his knee. The stone floor echoes as students and staff walk by on their way to lectures, lunch or home.

Jeremy Bentham was an early developer. In 1760, aged 12, he was sent to Queens College Oxford by his father to study law. He became so frustrated with the state of the English legal code that he decided to devote himself to critiquing and improving it, rather than practising it. He concentrated on developing objective standards for testing the usefulness of society's institutions, beliefs and ways of life. He is now most widely known for his doctrine of Utilitarianism, which declared that 'the greatest happiness of the greatest number' determined what was right in society. But he also wrote on many other subjects including religion, prison reform and animal welfare. His ideas continue to influence debate about social policy.

Bentham wanted his body to be as useful as possible after death. He strongly supported the dissection of corpses for the benefit of medical science, which at the time was regarded as a fate worse than death since dismemberment was thought to prevent the bodily resurrection. So in bequeathing his body to his friend Dr Southwood Smith he asked that it be used 'first to communicate curious interesting and highly important knowledge and secondly show that the primitive horror at dissection originates in ignorance... and that the human body when dissected instead of being an object of disgust is as much more beautiful than any other piece of mechanism as it is more curious and wonderful.' This was done, and Dr Smith delivered a lecture over Bentham's body at the Webb Street School of Anatomy and Medicine on the 'structure and functions of the human frame'.

But Bentham also asked that his body be displayed afterwards in a clearly labelled box wearing one of his suits in his chair with his stick nearby. It should be 'in the attitude in which I am sitting when engaged in thought [when] writing'. The auto-icon, he said in his will, could be present at any gatherings held by 'personal friends and other disciples' to commemorate him. This seems to have actually happened; a contemporary makes a jeering reference to meetings where the skeleton was present 'in order, we presume, that these Utilitarians may... cheat themselves into the belief that the father of their sect, though dead, yet speaketh'. Bentham also wrote a paper shortly before his death, envisaging (perhaps half-jokingly) that auto-iconism would 'supersede the necessity for sculpture' and auto-icons could be used by phrenologists to demonstrate how personality was linked to skull structure.

Bentham's auto-icon, or self-image, is now in the South Cloisters of UCL. His skeleton is surrounded with padding under the clothes. The head, which could not be properly preserved in the box, has been replaced by a wax model.

UCL exhibitions coordinator Susie Chan explained why she thinks people like the auto-icon.

> Bentham is one of the few things that permeates beyond the campus. People from outside the university have heard of him and come to see him. Also, you often see students showing Bentham to their parents. We do try and get people in off the street to look at our museums around campus, and we don't want people to feel that they can't walk in or don't know where they're going.
>
> I think it makes all the difference that it is actually his skeleton inside the clothes. People really like the fact that it's him – even though it's stuffing and not his head. His head used to be displayed with him, and sometimes people are disappointed it's not there anymore – but it's being looked after. It was quite a tempting thing for students to pinch. Also it does look quite gruesome. There's a photo on the touchscreen.
>
> We were thinking of ways of making the displays look more modern, and one idea was to take him out of his box. This

met with a resounding 'no' – people are very fond of him the way he is. So they shut him up at night and open him up in the morning, and it's part of the ritual of switching UCL on in the morning and shutting down at night.

We want to make sure he's there for the next 50-100 years, so we are going to stabilise the environment, take him out, give him a clean, make sure the light levels are fine and it's not too dusty.

The auto-icon attracts responses which are often playful. On top of the box the University's Bentham Project, part of its law faculty, has put a webcam they have nicknamed the PanoptiCam. This takes hourly snaps of people passing, both the name and function echoing Bentham's Panopticon, a design for a circular building which he envisaged as a prison in which inmates could be constantly observed. (The snaps are streamed on Twitter at @PanoptiStream).

One visitor to the auto-icon was the artist Shirin Homann-Saadat, based in Germany. She made a black slate box which was temporarily displayed next to it, inside which she put mini-models of the auto-icon box and of the Panopticon.

She told me about this work:

> Some people carry around first aid kits, others have make-up boxes. This is something like a portable 'Bentham-Essentials-Box', containing some biographical details, his Panopticon design, the auto-icon, as well as his basic ideas on who should be included in moral considerations and why.
>
> For the construction of the box I contracted a stone mason who mainly works on tombstones. I wanted it to have some epitaph-like qualities, because words carved into stone are serious and finite. It was important to me to focus on

Bentham's ideas, rather than 'iconising' him. So on the lid are carved his words about animals:

> *the question is not*
> *can they reason,*
> *nor, can they talk,*
> *but can they suffer*

and on the side:

> *We are under the governance*
> *of two sovereign masters:*
> *pain and pleasure.*

These thoughts of Bentham are important to me, because they open up the field of moral philosophy to animals, who can also suffer and feel pain and pleasure.

Including a model of the auto-icon and the Panopticon next to each other suggests that the concept of an auto-icon is not so different from that of a prison (many people build their own self-planned prisons to reach some form of immortality, don't they?). Bentham had more scientific ambitions in mind, but still, all these questions remain open when one sees the auto-icon.

Other aspects of the auto-icon intrigue me; Bentham didn't do it out of vanity but it's so vain – that mix is intriguing. It could also be seen as an altar to meditate about death – being present when you're not there, right down to your glasses and clothes.

The Living

CAN A MUSEUM CONTAIN LIVING THINGS, or does it then become a zoo, a laboratory, a theatre? When Francis Bacon listed the ideal collections of a prince in 1594, he excluded live things from the 'goodly huge cabinet' he recommended, admitting only things that 'want life and may be kept'. But his cabinet was complemented by live collections of rare beasts, birds and fish outside.

Some museums now bring those animals inside. For example, in its basement aquarium the Horniman Museum in south London displays a living coral reef. Behind the scenes they replicate daylight, temperature and lunar cycle from various places around the world so that corals will breed, and in 2015 carried out the first successful coral IVF in the UK. Gressenhall Farm and Workhouse in Norfolk is home to animal breeds common in the county a hundred years ago, such as Suffolk Punch horses and Norfolk Black turkeys.

Museums sometimes market themselves as 'living', usually on the strength of authentic settings or full-size replicas of places such as villages, farms or high streets and the use of costumed interpreters. So visitors can be customers in a 1940s-style sweetshop at the Milestones Museum of Living History in Basingstoke or see a working brass foundry at the Black Country Living Museum.

Beamish Open Air Museum in County Durham takes this approach one step further by running courses in period settings, including a 'heavy horse experience', and by teaching ploughing and tram driving.

Supporters of such approaches say that history needs to be taken off the page and many people, especially children, want to learn about history through doing rather than reading. Critics argue that history can never be accurately reconstructed. '"Living history" is an... ironic and misleading term in that it implies, on the one hand, that other forms of history are 'dead' and on the other, that one can bring history back to life by way of performance,' says Scott Magelssen, drama historian at the University of Washington. Others reject turning historical eras and ways of life into 'experiences' and wonder if they deprive people of the chance to use their own imaginations.

Do museums, then, risk losing their identity through admitting the living? By housing live animals, are they doing what zoos do, but not as well? By running courses and living history programmes, do they risk becoming impressive venues backed up by the kudos of being research institutions, instead of unique places for researching and displaying fragments of evidence in a relatively 'unprocessed' way? Or are such changes a healthy part of the continual self-reinvention which museums must undertake in order to compete with more dynamic forms of entertainment, make a difference to society and, not least, bring in income?

Live insects, plants and a human being feature in this section. In a corner of Liverpool World Museum, a micro environment has been built for a colony of leafcutter ants; at Charles Darwin's home in Kent the patch of earth where he experimented with weeds has been recreated as close as possible to its original spot. Lastly, live interpreter Andrew Ashmore patrols the deck of the Cutty Sark sailing ship in character as Captain Woodget. We listen to the captain and ask Andrew whether he considers himself an exhibit.

LEAFCUTTER ANTS

World Museum, Liverpool

PAUL FINNEGAN, TEAM LEADER at the World Museum's Bug House, has been showing me the live arachnids and insects stored in a back room, when he suddenly pulls a stick insect excitedly out of its box and squeezes its back end hard. 'Look!' he said, holding out a tiny black pellet in the palm of his hand. 'That's an egg. That'll take three years to hatch.' The insect leaps onto his chest and clings onto his Stranglers T-shirt. Paul seems happy – even proud – to be its perch.

Around us are Madagascan hissing cockroaches, a red rump tarantula, and a fat, silky, plump caterpillar – the Death's Head moth ('that's the one in *Silence of the Lambs*,' says Paul). Out front are more creatures – hermit crabs, emperor scorpions and a Giant Floridean Katydid with wings looking exactly like young waxy leaves.

Compared to these larger creatures, the ants do not immediately stand out. They walk along a thick vertical rope which runs out of some up-ended plastic sweet jars containing the nest, then horizontally above head height so people can watch their journey, then down again into a square metal box containing food. They emerge carrying petals, leaves or bits of fruit and retrace their steps back to the nest.

Biologist Richard Dawkins suggests that ants invented the town before humans did. Nests of leafcutter ants can be up to six metres deep and 20 metres in circumference, and are divided into chambers connected by tunnels. Worker ants find leaves, cut them up and bring the pieces to the nest, which contains the queen and larvae as well as the other workers. Some also bring droplets of water in their mouths. Inside the nest another type of worker ant, minims, cut the leaf fragments into tinier pieces. Others chew them to a pulp and still others excrete onto them to encourage fungus growth. This fungus is the ants' food, and can only flourish in the nests, which Dawkins therefore declares 'a true example of [plant] domestication by an agricultural species other than our own'.

It is this process, rather than any one particular creature, that is on display here. Paul told me more about this mini-ecosystem and how he maintains it.

> We acquired these ants from the late Professor David Stradling, Chairman of the board of trustees of Whitley Wildlife Conservation Trust, which owns Paignton Zoo. He studied the ants in Trinidad, at the William Beebe Tropical Research Station. We bought some workers and a queen, basically an egg-laying machine. They lay an egg every minute of their life, and they live for about 20 years.
>
> All the ants here are female. If the nest is large enough, the queen will lay lots of males and queens; a few of the males mate with a new queen then die. The queen stores the sperm in her body, which she can use to lay fertile eggs for the rest of her life. The queen who leaves takes a little bit of fungus in her mouth in a pouch like a hamster. She flies off, lands on the ground, digs a little burrow and starts another nest underground. I think there are about 30,000 ants here; if it gets to about 50,000 they will reproduce, but we can't have flying ants in the gallery. So I cull 100-200 workers each day by putting them in the freezer.
>
> We have to regulate everything for them; they're the most difficult thing we keep here. They should ideally be kept at 25.5°C. If the temperature goes above 27° or below 24° the colony will die off within a few days.
>
> A lot of them are carrying droplets of water in their mouths back into the nest to keep it almost saturated. And you'll

often see minims sitting on leaves when they're carried back by workers. They are protecting the ant carrying the leaf from parasitic wasps you get out in the rainforest which lay their eggs inside the ants. I'd love to spend several days and nights watching them, seeing what they do, but we can only stay here in the day.

I've been interested in nature since I was about three years old – first crabs and caterpillars, then birds, then amphibians and reptiles in my teens. I left school with no qualifications except Biology and English 'O' levels. I went on government training schemes and learned to become a painter and decorator, which I did for about 10 years.

When I was about 26 they opened a Natural History Centre here – stuffed and pickled animals, insects in drawers. I came for an interview for a six-week holiday job. I had to dash over from the hospital where my then girlfriend was giving birth to my eldest son – I was dripping with sweat, I'd left my tie on the train. I gave a talk on a barn owl. I used to keep one – I'd nursed it back to health after it had been shot, and trained it to fly to me. I was put on temporary contracts and eventually was made team leader when they opened the Bug House.

Live animals are a great teaching tool. It's all right having a dead or a stuffed animal in front of you but you can't see how it moves, how it behaves, how it smells. Plus, if you show children something live it grasps their attention. The ants are probably the most popular display in the whole museum. You'll get people saying 'why is this coming back with nothing? It's lazy.' It's like they see them as small humans almost.

DARWIN'S WEED GARDEN

Down House, Kent

'WHAT A SPLENDID PURSUIT Natural History would be if it was all observing and no writing,' sighed Charles Darwin in a letter to Joseph Hooker, the director of Kew Gardens, in February 1868. Darwin's book *The Variation of Plants and Animals under Domestication* had just been published; writing it had taken a toll on its author, who said it 'disgusted' him and was not worth a fifth of the effort it had taken.

By then Darwin was living at Down House in Kent, where he carried out much of his nature observation after returning in 1836 from his voyage around the world on 'The Beagle'. He lived there with his family for 40 years and observed and experimented with orchids, earthworms and other plants and animals. One small experiment involved weeds. Working with his children's governess Catherine Thorley, he cleared a small patch of ground, and in 1857 and again in 1858 they inserted wires where seedlings were growing, pulled out the wires of those which died and counted them. Darwin summarised the findings in his most important work, *On the Origin of Species*, in Chapter 3, 'Struggle for Existence'. Here he was wondering what stopped plant or animal species increasing, and at which stage of life:

> Eggs or very young animals seem generally to suffer most, but this is not invariably the case. With plants there is a vast destruction of seeds, but, from some observations which I have made, I believe that it is the seedlings which suffer most from germinating in ground already thickly stocked with other plants. Seedlings, also, are destroyed in vast numbers by various enemies; for instance, on a piece of ground three feet long and two feet wide, dug and cleared,

> and where there could be no choking from other plants, I marked all the seedlings of our native weeds as they came up, and out of 357 no less than 295 were destroyed, chiefly by slugs and insects.

He goes on to say that if mown or cropped grass is left to grow, 'more vigorous plants gradually kill the less vigorous', even if the latter are more fully grown.

Down House is now a museum and the weed garden is outside its main entrance and gift shop. It is a tiny, unassuming bed protected by a twig fence next to an overgrown orchard. When I visited in August 2014 it contained dead leaves, a nettle, a rosebay willow herb plant, pebbles, and a low shrub or two. No one was looking at it. Elsewhere in the garden are larger, well-tended, clearly labelled beds of rhubarb, pumpkins, endive, radish, cabbage, beetroot, parsley, chicory and other fruit and vegetables. There are also the sites of some of Darwin's other experiments and the sand walk, 'his 'thinking path', where he strolled to work out his ideas.

English Heritage repeated Darwin's experiment at the site in 2005, finding that more than three fifths of the seedlings survived, whereas Darwin's showed that just under one sixth survived when he carried it out.

Professor David Kohn is director of the American Museum of Natural History's Darwin Manuscripts Project, which has made many of Darwin's papers available online. He also curated the exhibition 'Darwin's Garden: An Evolutionary Adventure' at the museum in 2008. He outlined what Darwin wanted to achieve with the weed garden and introduced its importance in the development of Darwin's thinking.

> At this point Darwin is writing what's called the long version of *On the Origin of Species*, and he wants to see if he can demonstrate aspects of his theory. I don't think in one experiment you could demonstrate the whole of natural

selection, which has lots of different parts, but basically the weed garden shows the considerable death rate of the seedlings, and he tries to figure out why they die. He's seeing how selection occurs. He has the view that certain parts of life are more crucial than others, and for plants it's the seedling stage, so he's got to focus in on that.

It's what ecologists would call a quadrat today. As an experiment it's interesting, because he's giving a lot of attention to controlling parameters. So he puts a fence round to deter large animals and measures what happens regularly. It's a real focus on elements which might cause death – slugs, the heat of the sun and so on.

The weed garden experiments focus on one point in the process of competition and jostling among organisms. Darwin is also very interested in what we call 'buried viable seeds'. The whole premise of the experiment is that if you clear the ground, this very viable seed will pop up, which you will have a window on. He also has a notion of 'preoccupation of land'– you have a different result if you start with the putative loser which is well-established on the land. It's symptomatic of the rich things he's thinking.

Darwin has a problem in presenting his theory in that a lot of things he'd like to know haven't been studied. There are some analogues among agronomists experimenting with different grasses, but that's about it. So he has to invent these sketches for experiments and hope it will convey a sense of what he's talking about and give it some scientific structure. They're part of the process of constructing the *Origin* as a narrative.

He's got most of his theory of natural selection structured in 1838-9, and written in 1842 and 44. But from 1854-7 he's struggling to define the mechanism by which species are made. The principle of divergence is the most important concept he developed in the 1850s, and that's what is at stake in the weed garden and other experiments. He believes species can be made by intense competition, even when organisms aren't separated geographically, something which is controversial to this day.

There's another experiment run in parallel in another part of the garden, called the long plot. There, he does the opposite to the weed garden. Instead of clearing the area, he doesn't let the gardener mow the lawn. 'How much life can this support?' he asks.

And in 1855 he had dug up a quadrat in the field to the right of the sand walk. There, he and the children's nurse looked at how many different kinds of things are growing together – he has the idea that more life will be produced if there are more species growing together, an early statement of the principle of biodiversity.

And then he gets interrupted by Alfred Russel Wallace's paper which also suggests species are formed by natural selection, then when the shock wears off he starts writing the *Origin*, and after that he doesn't have time for those experiments any more. The experiments he does after the *Origin* are totally different. After it's published he starts a massive experiment programme in the grounds of Down House, focusing on specific adaptations – pollinators, the structure of flowers, climbing plants, things in human behaviour, expressions of emotion. That is marked by extreme rigour and repetition upon repetition. But the pre-*Origin* experiments are very playful – I am fond of them.

It's important to recreate Darwin's garden the way it was because the goal is educational, both of the spirit and of youngsters' minds. If it can be done powerfully and cleverly enough, perhaps we can get students to understand experientially how Darwin thought. As a historian of science I don't separate the manuscripts and what he did. Darwin was a very English scientist – he didn't need a laboratory. He makes the world around him into his field station.

Captain Woodget

The Cutty Sark, London

CAPTAIN WOODGET IS BUSY fielding questions. A man asks how 'The Cutty Sark' used to get up the Thames to the docks. 'You need a pilot boat sir,' replies the captain. A small child, worried about the ship sinking, is reassured: 'We'll go in those two small boats that you see there – they're our lifeboats. You'll find water, and charts, and compasses, and rations. Don't you worry, I've never been down in any ship, so you're safe with me.' 'Why was it called a poop deck?' '*Puppis* is Latin for back, the stern of the ship. It's nothing to do with poo.' Another story: 'Now our cook – there's an interesting man. Looks like a Chinaman, cooks like an Englishman. Abandoned as a baby – he was adopted.' Girls are told they can't sign up as apprentices, but then hear the story of Hannah Snell who joined the Royal Navy by pretending to be a man. The captain talks statistics while directing our gaze up to the mast and along the decks, then takes off his hat to solemnly remember two men swept overboard.

'Gone for all eternity. Doyle couldn't even swim.' Then come instructions for knocking weevils out of ships' biscuits.

The ship is named after the witch Nannie Dee in Robert Burns's 1791 poem *Tam o' Shanter*. Nannie Dee wore a short ('cutty' in Scots) linen undergarment ('sark') which Tam enjoyed watching her dancing in. The figurehead indeed shows the witch bare breasted, wearing a scrap of cloth. The ship was built as a tea clipper, but switched to carrying wool from Australia when steamships started to take over the tea trade and the opening of the Suez Canal made voyage times to China much shorter. Woodget skippered the ship from 1885 to 1895, producing stunning passage times between Australia and Britain. The ship was sold to Portugal in 1895 and renamed *Ferreira*.

Andrew Ashmore plays the captain regularly on the ship at Greenwich on the south bank of the Thames. His other roles include Pythagoras, Hans Sloane, and Darius King of Persia. He has also put on 'Tales from Troy' (a condensed version of *The Iliad*) at the British Museum in three 20-minute plays, with the judgement of Paris presented in the style of Blind Date. His longest-running show is the Domesday book at the National Archives which has been going for 15 years.

Andrew spoke to me while changing out of his costume in a back office immediately after his turn on the ship.

> It was a really exhilarating day today – we had everything from little kids to old sailors. There were two older chaps trying to get me out of character, but I wouldn't, and they enjoyed that; one person even came up to me at the end and asked me to sign a book with Captain Woodget's signature.
>
> I use a Norfolk accent for the captain because he's from there, and I've had quite a few people from that area. A person once said to me 'I saw your grave yesterday', which

was a strange opening remark. He just wanted to let me know he knew who I was playing. I just replied: 'I haven't been feeling too badly lately sir'. I've got a beard today which I don't usually have but I grew it for the captain, otherwise I wouldn't be him, it wouldn't feel right.

A lot of it's picking your character. When we started on this job we were asked to do the Portuguese captain since the ship was sold to the Portuguese afterwards. But I said I didn't want to do that – it wasn't a particularly good period for the ship and what we've got here is looking back on the height of the tea trade, the height of the wool trade.

The stories we tell on 'The Cutty Sark' are all true. Research is absolutely key – here there's a vast archive with photos of the ship, the ship's log, apprentices' letters. We have letters from one of the captain's sons, who was an apprentice – the language of the time is wonderful and very evocative. And the ship is such a fantastic object – you can see the masts, you can be in the hold, you can be in the 'tween decks.

First you work with curators and education staff to decide what the key things are that you want to get across. It's a very exciting time when you are starting on the research and you're absorbing new information like blotting paper. Live interpreters often over-prepare at the beginning – there's that fear of being caught out, of Jeremy Paxman being your first visitor. But after a short time you get to know what the visitors want to learn about the site or exhibition. And then you really hope that you can go off more at a tangent sometimes, that someone's going to ask you something a bit more obscure.

The key thing is to make people feel very comfortable, and if you're going to ask them questions at the beginning to keep them really simple, like 'what do you think of the weather today?', or 'how did you get here?', to get them to relax into talking to you, then bring them into the world of the character, for example 'would you feel comfortable climbing that high?', and so forth, to really get them to connect emotionally rather than in an intellectual and abstract way.

When you really get into a character as I've done with Major Wade, who I've been playing for 12 years at the Cabinet War Rooms, I know his reactions and opinions sometimes almost better than my own. It's like putting on an old and very comfortable pair of shoes. So I can give an informed answer to questions which are a matter of opinion, where there is no right answer.

Ten or 15 years ago you could quite easily drive people out of galleries by being big and actor-ish (never a good thing), but now people are so used to live interpretation, they're more likely to come straight up to you and say 'who are you then, what do you know'?

We're not exhibits, but we're part of the interpretation. Interactives break, but we don't. Hopefully we're the most interactive thing there is – we can follow any train of thought, hopefully answer any questions and make visitors feel that they're a part of history through the character we choose.

Babylonian map of the world
British Museum

The Extinct

WHEN THE TRADESCANTS gathered plants and seeds from around the world to sit alongside the curiosities in their 'Ark', extinction was an unknown concept and species conservation not a reason for collecting. French naturalist George Cuvier is credited with establishing extinction of animal species as a fact when he outlined the concept in a lecture to the Institut Francais in Paris in 1796, after he had examined some fossil skeletons and became convinced they could not come from living animals.

Now scientists think that over 99% of all plant and animal species which have ever lived on Earth are extinct, and that there have been at least five mass extinctions (defined as an event where over 75% of species die out) during Earth's history. We are now in the middle of the sixth extinction, according to palaeontologist Richard Leakey and science writer Roger Lewin – and its cause is obvious. 'For each of the Big Five [extinctions] there are theories of what caused them, some of them compelling, but none proven,' they say. 'For the sixth extinction, however, we do know the culprit. We are.'

One modern conservation scheme which aims to slow down or even stop this sixth extinction, Frozen Ark, was set up in 1996 to save and freeze tissue from endangered animals containing their

DNA. Some museums are also involved in animal conservation. Live jewel-coloured Costa Rican frogs sit on bromeliad lilies in Manchester Museum's Vivarium, and species of frog which have never been bred in captivity elsewhere hatch out inside the tanks. It is also working with organisations including the Horniman Museum to try to save the endangered Lemur Leaf frog.

Naturally, museums are more likely to be sanctuaries for artefacts than for animals – not only documents and objects but even music, sounds and digital 'objects'. Museums Association guidelines for acquiring and caring for objects sound as strict as any code for conserving wildlife or natural habitats. Museums should not accept objects if they suspect they have been 'stolen, illegally excavated or removed from a monument, site or wreck' since 1970, the date of a United Nations Educational, Scientific and Cultural Organisation (UNESCO) convention on cultural property ownership. They must 'protect all items from loss, damage and physical deterioration' as well as fire, flood and vandalism. Objects should only be sold as a last resort, and then not for short-term profit, not if they are part of the museum's core collection, and if it improves public access to them. More widely, museums should uphold environmental protection treaties and 'prevent abuse of places of scientific, historical or cultural importance'. The code is not legally binding, but museums risk damaging their reputations and losing funding if they do not try to follow it.

Of course, conserving objects is different to conserving wildlife or natural habitats. Remedial conservation involves repairing objects unobtrusively; preventative conservation regulates environmental conditions such as light and humidity and controls pests. Once a museum accepts an object, enormous amounts of money, time and painstaking care can be spent on preserving it. I remember listening to a V&A conservator describing the hours she had spent on dying thread so it exactly matched existing thread on a medieval quilt she was working on – and this was before she had even started sewing.

It is worth asking what exactly is being conserved. How does artefact preservation relate to saving languages, ways of life, even whole civilisations? When the last 38 inhabitants of the remote Scottish island of St Kilda were permanently evacuated in 1930, the household objects changed their nature as soon as the islanders' way of life ended, becoming no more than 'curios' and 'relics' for the watching journalist from the *Glasgow Herald*: 'The churns are curios and the hand mills are with the collectors. St Kilda is of the historied past,' he wrote melodramatically. The islanders hoped to make a profit from them, he added: 'Many were wholly unsentimental about selling their distinctive spinning wheels and oil cruses to those desperate for relics from this unique outpost of civilisation. One put a sign in the window of an abandoned house: St Kilda relics for sale. Apply within.' St Kilda is now a UNESCO World Heritage site.

An extinct animal, civilisation and practice are represented in this section. The animal is the quagga, from the plains of Africa; the civilisation is ancient Babylon, from what is now the Middle East; and the practice is flittin' (transporting) peat on the Scottish island of Fetlar, in the Shetlands. The only one of these which has even a slim chance of returning is the quagga – if scientists of the future are able to clone animals from DNA and think it makes sense to do so. The Babylonian clay tablet in this section leads us to yet another ark, one of the earliest – that of the Biblical flood story.

QUAGGA SKELETON

Grant Museum of Zoology, London

IT IS A SLIGHTLY GHOULISH PLEASURE to wander among the polished wood cases in the Grant Museum and encounter the structures and textures of the preserved creatures and the strange meetings between them which emerge. A tiny infant furless rabbit is tilted diagonally onto its head in a bottle; its flat back paws will never be big enough to show their function as launch pads. The brown striped fur of a curled up thylacine, or Tasmanian Tiger, brushes the edges of a large jar. Grinning primate skeletons stare down from the mezzanine (I happened to be visiting on Halloween, and wondered at first if they had been put there for the occasion). This museum is more like a cabinet of curiosities than any I have come across so far.

I start reading labels, and learn that the siphonophora (for example the Portuguese Man-of-War) is, or are, colonies of zooids which can only survive if they act as one organism. Another creature, the remora, attaches itself to whales and sharks using the suckers on its head, saving energy which would otherwise be spent on swimming. And indeed its head has a flattened surface, looking strangely like a shower nozzle.

A small picture of Robert Grant, the first holder of a chair of Zoology and Comparative Anatomy in the UK, is partly hidden behind the greyish papery skin of the reproductive organs of a platypus, its fallopian tubes recognisable. Grant, who was one of Darwin's early mentors, founded the museum for teaching purposes in 1827.

The museum's quagga skeleton – one of only seven which exist anywhere – stands in an 'Extinct and Endangered' case near the entrance, along with fossil fish, a Japanese giant salamander and an elephant tusk with bullet holes (the elephant was poached).

Quaggas, a type of zebra native to Africa with stripes only on the front halves of their bodies, became extinct in 1883 through hunting and the use of their habitats for livestock farming. However, this was not the end of the quaggas' story. In 1980 a German taxidermist called Reinhold Rau was remounting three quaggas which had been stuffed in the 19th century when he found muscle and connective tissue on the skins. He alerted scientists to these, and the samples were found to contain DNA.

In 1984 the quagga became the first extinct animal to have its DNA partially sequenced, by Russell Higuchi and colleagues at the University of California, Berkeley. This made scientists wonder whether extinct animals could be brought back through cloning. Less dramatically, this sequencing showed that the quagga was closely related to the plains zebra, probably a subspecies of it. Three years later Rau started to selectively breed plains zebras to produce offspring which look exactly like quaggas, a project which continues. Scientists disagree about whether these are the genuine creature. (The extinct quaggas may have been different to the current ones because of adaptations to their particular habitat, which was more arid than that of the plains zebra).

Even so, these newly-bred quaggas could allow scientists to understand the function of stripes – they may repel flies or help to regulate body temperature. (If an animal has stripes on only one part of its body, scientists should easily be able to compare the two parts). Biologist Peter Heywood from Rhode Island's Brown University even argues that returning quaggas to their natural habitat could be part of righting historical wrongs in South Africa.

Grant curator Mark Carnall describes how the skeleton entered the museum and talks more broadly about the idea of bringing extinct animals back to life by using their DNA.

> A quagga looks like half horse, half zebra. That's one of the most interesting things about them. In the wild they would

have behaved like other species and subspecies of zebra, so pottering around, grazing, running away from things occasionally!

In 1972 the Grant had what it thought were two zebra skeletons. A zoologist called Alan Gentry became interested in them, and identified one as a donkey – rather a downgrade in interest – but the other turned out to be a quagga, which makes it one of the rarest skeletons in the world. It had been acquired for teaching at a time when it wasn't too important where it came from – these specimens were treated very much how you'd imagine lab equipment is treated today. Whereas today, context is all important – we want to know what the animal was doing, what altitude they were, we'd want their six-figure grid reference.

It isn't quite as popular as some of our other highlight specimens, things like the thylacine and the dodo. The dodo of course is an icon for extinction and there is a growing awareness about the thylacine.

Unfortunately, the quagga skeleton looks like a horse. It doesn't have that visual impact of 'this is something weird and wonderful that we no longer have.' But we've got a model in there showing its stripes and patternation which we desperately try to point people to. Also, the quagga is a subspecies and doesn't quite have the same pull as a species. This is very much true with modern-day animal conservation – if you're using the word 'sub' it sounds like a second-class citizen which we shouldn't be too worried about.

The possibility of bringing extinct animals back to life is an interesting area, and for museums and scientists it's a great way to have discussions around extinction and our responsibility towards extinct organisms. But we're very far away from doing what you'd expect from science fiction films – take your hair and grow it in a test tube and that's the new you. There have been a couple of extinct species that have been sort of brought back. A subspecies of ibex was 'brought back' for seven minutes and then it died.

And of course where do we put these things? One of the reasons they may be extinct is because their environments disappeared, so we'd have to create that environment, and then there's loads of things we don't know the answers to – how many individuals do you need to make a sustainable population? What if the animal we bring back has a genetic disease?

Another problem with cloning is modern diseases. All the animals that are around today are in an arms race with viruses and pollution levels and climate. An animal from the past wouldn't be adapted to combat these. So I can imagine on the day you do release a quagga into the wild, it would take two steps and keel over and die from a hundred and five different diseases.

And should we be investing resources in coming up with these monster things that look like extinct animals but aren't, when at the moment we are losing species before we have even described them?

It's important to see the quagga skeleton and remains of other recently extinct animals, because it's different to reading a news story about endangered animals. When you are confronted with something in a museum it can be quite an intimate relationship. You might see remains of obscure animals, or those that are in far-flung places of the world (extinction is happening pretty much daily – some of it's our fault, some of it isn't). By seeing and having that personal relationship, hopefully that message is much more effective.

BABYLONIAN MAP OF THE WORLD

British Museum, London

THE NAMES OF LONG-EXTINCT empires, kingdoms, city states and peoples haunt rooms 54 to 56 of the British Museum. Assyria, Babylonia, Mesopotamia; Hittites, Sumerians, Kassites. The division into rooms tries to help us make sense of history in the Near and Middle East by separating the civilisations and literally walking the visitor through them. In fact, these rooms themselves have become an inextricable part of these civilisations for me, so that I think of the Assyrians and Babylonians as 'museum-y' or at least only to be understood properly through careful curation and scholarship.

Room 55 shows Mesopotamia from 1500 to 539 BC. Mesopotamia means 'between two rivers' and is a region between the Tigris and Euphrates, now modern Iraq and eastern Syria. Babylonia was south Mesopotamia. Even within this period there is a complex succession of empires and peoples in the area. The Babylonian empire of this time grew up after about 1250 BC when the Assyrian kingdom exerted its authority over Mesopotamia and as far south as Egypt. A few place names on the wall map – Nineveh, Tyre, Sidon – ring a bell with me, presumably from vague memories of the Old Testament.

The Babylonian map of the world sits in its own case in the middle of the room, as small as the palm of my hand. It was made in about 700-500 BC and is so fragile that it is never lent to other museums and only rarely moved from its case. It hasn't even been kiln-fired, which is usually done to clay tablets to make them last longer. In his book *The Ark before Noah*, from which the information about the tablet here is largely taken, the British Museum's Assistant Keeper of the Department of the Middle East Irving Finkel explains that it is 'the world's oldest usable map' and one of the most remarkable cuneiform tablets ever discovered.

On the front are lines of tiny cuneiform script. A diagram below shows a circle with eight triangles around the rim, like a stylised sun. Inside the circle are two horizontal rectangles, joined by two slightly curving vertical lines. This shows the heartland of Mesopotamia – the known world, to those who drew it. The upper rectangle represents Babylon, which is the centre of this world; the dot in the rectangle's centre represents the capital city and is probably ruler Nebuchadnezzar's ziggurat. The river Euphrates flows south to the other rectangle, whose right end is marked 'marsh' and the left 'outflow'. This rectangle approximates to the Persian Gulf.

The reverse of the tablet explains some of the diagram's features. The outer circle is the limit of the known world, which is marked by a ring of 'bitter water'. The triangles are mountains, or nagûs, just beyond this circle. Wonderful things can be found on them. On the third nagû there are 'winged birds [which] cannot flap their own wings', and oxen which can run fast enough to catch wild animals. On the fourth can be found giant pieces of wood, 'as thick as a parsiktu-vessel'. Finkel suggests these are the ribs of the Ark which has come to rest on the mountain after the flood, basing this claim on a correlation between the description of the pieces of wood here and similar words in another account of the Babylonian flood myth on an older tablet. In fact, it is likely that the flood story in the book of Genesis originated with the Babylonians and was adapted by the Judaeans, who shared the land with them.

Finkel says he comes from a 'daft family where museums and galleries were an essential thing' and has been fascinated with cuneiform since he was an undergraduate. His discussion of the tablet highlights connections between Babylonian beliefs and those of other civilisations, thus crossing some of the boundaries implied by the museum's room divisions.

> The known world was visualised as a flat circle – whether they saw the world as a disc or a ball we do not know. And if you reached the perimeter of the known world you reached the bank of the bitter river or sea. This was perfectly rational because if you go far enough you hit water and you do see the horizon as a line, so that at a simple level this was not so bizarre.
>
> There are places dotted around in the landscape which are more or less right but they're not perfect. Quite a lot of people who have written about it have been critical, as if it's inaccurate or sloppy. This is an absurdity because the preoccupation of the scribe who wrote it down was not the known world within the ring, but the world beyond it. The real principle is to anchor in position some of the heroes and important things in mythology and odd things that were to be seen if you went far enough. It's an attempt to bring a lot of disparate material under control. This knowledge derives from a period a millennium or more older than the tablet itself. So it's a compilation of older traditions – a compendium of information.
>
> We know that at the time there were people who went on very long travel expeditions, mostly for commerce. Already in the third millennium people went as far as India and traded with people in the Indus Valley. And probably there were always a certain number of people prepared to go out

in a caravan and be away for several years hunting for jewels or things that would make their fortune, or they were impelled by curiosity, or they were loners.

So some of these stories encapsulate travellers' tales. In one of the triangles, for example, there are large birds that do not fly and we know there are such things in the world; although you can't readily find the trees with jewels on them, you can imagine how such a story might develop. There would be a cycle of stories, a bit like *The Odyssey* perhaps. It's an attempt to harmonise traditions like this with a certain amount of astronomical and geographical knowledge.

The Babylonian flood story is influenced by their dependency on two massive rivers. This meant that the destructive power of water and potential for flooding, as well as its benefits for irrigation, was a daily part of their lives.

Greek tradition also saw the world as surrounded with a sea, very similar to the Babylonian conception. I think the stimulus for the Greek conception of the world in its outer function was almost certainly borrowed from a Babylonian forerunner. There is probably a continuum of this sort of map which comes right down to the Middle Ages and ends up in those drawings which say 'here be monsters' and so on.

I think that the flood story of the Babylonians was irresistible to the Judaean poets who produced the Biblical account. It exemplifies nature as a tool of God, the vulnerability of man, and how swift and unrelenting retribution can be. However, in the Judaean theological framework the story became moral and educational – the flood was punishment for evildoing.

The idea that a topic in Holy Writ can be shown to be derived from something else is a thing which many people find objectionable. But it's not so complicated to accept if you regard it as a literary device. The original story may have had potency but in new hands it is even more potent and lent itself very well to their idea of punishment for sin.

One could hope that sooner or later someone will uncover a duplicate because the flood story is part of a Mesopotamian literary tradition that was copied and recopied in school. So at any time you might have 20 or 30 examples of a particular composition in different libraries or houses.

Cuneiform was used for Sumerian and Babylonian especially. Many countries in the Middle East adopted it to write their own languages and this happened because many kings and city states wanted to have their own writers and the only people who could write used cuneiform. So it was used for Hittite, Elamite, Persian and other languages.

You have this rather interesting situation of quite a complicated, hard to learn writing system running uninterruptedly for at least 3000 years, and also being adopted by other nations whose languages were unrelated. The appearance of the alphabet in about 1000 BC didn't dislodge cuneiform entirely for at least a millennium afterwards.

Babylon fell in 539 BC to Cyrus king of Persia, and the Persians took over. They used Aramaic as their language of administration, and Babylonian began to be squeezed out. People spoke Aramaic – Jesus, for example, grew up speaking Aramaic.

Cuneiform died out by the second century AD. But for three millennia you had had a very effective cycle of cultures and empires in Mesopotamia which rose and fell but all lived in the same landscape with the same written language – pretty successful really.

BENDS FOR PEAT FLITTIN'

Fetlar Interpretive Centre, Shetland

FETLAR, the fourth largest Shetland Island, has gentle green curves and sandy beaches. The volunteer-run Interpretive Centre is housed in a small white building with a colourful mural on one wall, next to a telephone box in the only village of any size on the island, Houbie.

Fewer than 100 people now live there, a situation which residents are trying to change through regeneration projects and advertising. 'Fetlar has an eclectic mix of housing, ranging from large lairds' houses to small two-room crofters' cottages,' declares the island's main website. The Interpretive Centre plays its part in presenting Fetlar as an attractive island with a history. One exhibition was on Sir William Watson Cheyne, from one of the island's two laird families, a campaigner in the late 19th century for the antiseptic surgery techniques he had learned by working with medical pioneer Joseph Lister.

Peat flitting dates from a time when lairds and crofters comprised most of Fetlar's society. The best peat was on Lambhoga peninsula in the south-west of the island. Small farms, or crofts, stood on the peninsula before they were cleared in the enclosure programme of the laird Sir Arthur Nicolson in the 1820s ('he comes across as a ruthless landowner who evicted his tenants,' says the trust which now runs the Nicolson family home). Each croft had paid rent, which included the right to cut peat for fuel, and this right continued when the families were forced elsewhere. So through the 19th century and until the 1950s the islanders would cut slabs of peat each summer and transport ('flit') it back to their homes by boat or horse.

The families would travel to Lambhoga in early July and settle down in peat houses, setting up beds, lighting fires and putting bottles of milk into the cool peat banks. Peat houses had turf walls, roofs of wooden planks covered with turf and perhaps an old sail to keep out water. The house was mainly used as a sleeping space which everyone shared – beds were wooden planks on turf, covered with straw or heather and blankets.

They would get up at 2 or 3 o'clock each morning, cut slabs of peat and load them on the horses. These were led to peat stacks nearby or loaded onto boats and rowed to the other side of the island if families lived there. The lairds and the minister could afford to pay adults to cut and bring peat; crofters could not, but would sometimes pay peat boys and girls, who could be as young as nine.

'Bends' was the equipment used to fasten kishies (baskets) full of peat onto the horses. The museum displays a set and sells a booklet from where the crofters' quotes here are taken. The saddling technique has a very particular vocabulary:

'The flakki was a straw blanket covered by a hessian bag which was placed directly on the back of the mare. On top of this sat the klibber, a wooden "saddle" with crossed wooden hooks on top. And on top of the klibber went the maishie, a kind of net made of coir. The peat kishies were supple straw baskets, one on each side of the mare – they were held in place by the crossed hooks of the klibbers, and the maishie was wrapped around them to hold them fast. The flakki was held in place by the wimgirt, a strap which went under the belly of the mare. The tailgirt, another strap which went under the tail of the mare to ensure stability, was heavily padded to protect the animal. The mares were led by means of a halter.'

Most people remember the hardship of peat cutting, but some also remember fun and practical jokes. On one occasion dead sheep were pushed down chimneys and doors closed so that workers choked on smoke. The cutters would sometimes go to July dances at Leagarth, Sir Watson Cheyne's home.

Peat flitting on Fetlar ended in the 1950s, when other types of fuel took over and the peninsula's peat started to run out, as islander Charlie Thomason remembers: 'Tak da toon o Helliersness [part of the peninsula]– it wis a fair lump o gründ du knows– an it wis cut clean aff o da face o da earth in a matter o thirty year.'

Peat flitter Joan Coutts remembers taking clothes over to the peninsula, the houses they stayed in, and some of the jokes:

> Well yon wis wir summer work when we were young, an I can tell you it wis a very happy time we hed. I look back on it wi fond memories. We hed kishies opő da mares du sees...wi food i dem, bedclaise i dem, an wir ain claise at we wir gyaan ta were, an juist a lot of things–toowels an aa. Da Barn wis a lovely hoose, I mind dat. Tommy Garriock stayed dere, an Willie an Magnie Bruce, an Liza an aa dem. You gőed ta bed an kept aa your claise on. He [the bed] took up da half o da room... an everybody gőed in him–just da whole lot.
>
> Wis young lads wid rig wis up–dress wis up wi different claise–an maybe come awaa runnin through hooses. We wir young an we wid hev a peerie spree maybe...Da lasses wid pit on da men's claise an da men wid pit on da lasses claise... An dere wis Yell eens at cam ower...dey wid play pranks du sees... aa kind o fun–dey wir nae ill at aa. An dey wid tak wir bottles o milk–we put it doon i da grund an laid

feals ower it ta keep it fresh–an dan da boys wid come upő da night an dey wid drink it.

Katy Jackson managed the Fetlar Interpretive Centre, where some of the equipment is displayed, between 2011 and 2014. She describes the work and explains why peat flittin' remains important.

> I went to Shetland because I really wanted a change of scene. I come from Kent, a very built-up place, and I was at a stage of life where I longed for peace and quiet, fewer people, and Fetlar certainly gave me that.
>
> As manager I was the only paid member of staff so it was everything from meeter-greeter to floor-washer to toilet-cleaner to curator! The museum had been lovingly and carefully set up 20 years previously, but it needed refreshing. I'm not from a history background but I am very good at displaying and doing lots of stuff for not very much money. Myself and a group of volunteers completely redecorated the interior, redisplayed all the objects and set up a craft shop so that local people could sell their goods there.
>
> Peat flitting is now passing out of living memory in Fetlar. It is from a time when the year revolved around your connection with the land, with farming, food, keeping yourself warm; literally in Shetland, making hay while the sun shines. Those few fleeting months in the summer when the weather is good are very precious. It was also something that adults and children did together, and was one of the last times that Shetland ponies were used for work purposes.
>
> Visitors to the centre are a mixture of tourists and local people. For people who live on the island, the museum has a social function. When I was there people would come down for a cup of tea and a chat; you'd get kids coming in

after school to buy sweets. Sometimes people would bring objects in.

People who live in Fetlar are very proud of the museum; it displays their histories, and has photographs of old familiar friends; local people like to pop in for five minutes and watch a clip of the archive film. 'There's Lee,' they'd say, 'there's so and so'. The pride is not untinged with poignancy because a lot of these remote crofting communities have had big population loss over the years; and the museum captures some of the older and better days in people's eyes.

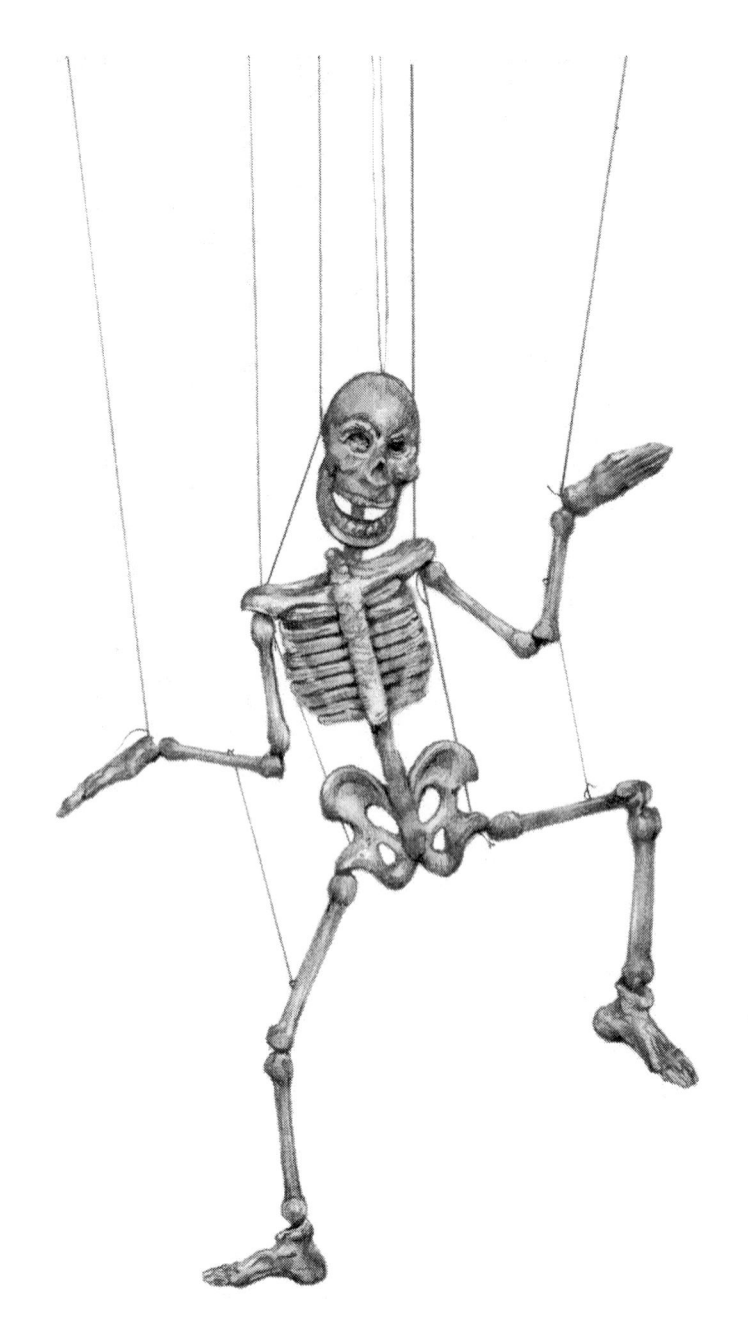

Marionette
Victoria and Albert Museum

The Mobile

IN MANCHESTER MUSEUM in 2013, a 4000-year old Egyptian statuette of a man called Neb-Senu started rotating slowly and spookily on its base, turning through about 200° in seven days. It was good publicity for the museum (news items appeared mentioning ancient curses) but nevertheless had to be stopped; movement involves friction and invites damage, and a museum's first duty is to its objects. Filming by the museum revealed that the statue rotated more during the day, and the cause was tracked down to vibrations from traffic and visitors walking past. Neb-Senu is now safely stationary, though he can still be seen rotating on the web.

Museums are at a disadvantage, though, in a world full of fast-paced multimedia. Static objects often demand slow and sometimes effortful looking and understanding, without the immediate appeal of animation. Is it even possible to appreciate transport, clothes, machinery, animals, if they do not move? To tackle this problem, museums may show complementary films, use replicas or even operate some objects occasionally. But stasis does have its compensations – one could argue, as taxidermist Jeremy Adams does when talking about the stuffed barn owl in this book, that static objects can be studied more closely and for longer.

Mobility is central to the three objects here – a marionette, a helicopter and a mechanical model for demonstrating light waves. But even for these exhibits, logistical and conservation demands hold sway. The marionette dances occasionally, the helicopter is the only one in its museum which flies, and the wave machine, like Neb-Senu, moves only on the web.

Marionette

Theatre and Performance Collections,
Victoria and Albert Museum

In the V&A's Theatre and Performance Collections, costumes worn by Dame Edna Everage and Adam Ant stand in a ghostly half-light; mini models of stage sets are tilted and lit to show the Forest of Arden and Hamlet's Elsinore; posters advertise long-finished productions; and you can turn a handle on a rattle machine to make the noise of a storm for the stage. The marionette shares a shelf with film clips of Royal Shakespeare Company performances from where, with a naughty grin, it ambushes you like skeletons in churches designed to remind you of your mortality.

The puppet was part of the Tiller-Clowes troupe, one of the last Victorian marionette troupes in England, in the 1860s or 1870s. Many people couldn't get to theatres, so groups took plays on the road and might put on three or four short plays or music hall turns in one day, along with a pantomime. Popular choices were *Maria*

Marten, based on the true story of a Suffolk woman murdered by her fraudster lover, or *Lady Audley's Secret*, based on the sensation novel about a bigamous woman who abandons her baby, pushes one of her husbands down a well and tries to murder one of his friends.

The V&A's curator of popular entertainment, Catherine Haill, describes the atmosphere of those performances and the role that the skeleton might have played in them:

> Fairgrounds were huge business and it was wonderful when a fairground came to your area. There were circus tents, barkers announcing the show, and brass brand musicians.
>
> This skeleton would have been part of a warm-up musical or variety set of acts. Anything that made a hit on the main stage was reproduced as soon as possible by marionette people. So, for example in the collection we've got a marionette who juggles with his feet with a great big pole, and this was after somebody called the Great Polanda had a hit at Sadler's Wells in the 19th century. In the same display case in the V&A we've got a tightrope walker who was based on Chevalier Blondin, a hugely famous tightrope walker in the 1860s.
>
> The skeleton would have been reproducing some kind of harlequinade act on the halls, where there was always a lot of fun to be made from one thing transforming into another. This one is wonderful because it comes on and can dance as a skeleton made up together, but the next minute all the bones fly apart.
>
> They were done with music – it would have gone right the way through any kind of Victorian performance, much as it goes through film now. And you'd have had music which was sympathetic to this act, so perhaps slow music at the

beginning and then there'd be a crescendo when the skeleton burst apart.

It was for everybody, not just children – it's only in the 20th century that puppetry is thought of as something for a younger audience. People had a far less sophisticated sense of humour in the 19th century than we do now and a marionette act like this would have been absolutely hilarious. And people were far more used to death than we are now. Most people in the 18th and 19th centuries would have been familiar with dead bodies – children would have seen their brothers and sisters dead. An image of a skeleton would have been less taboo.

The shows were hugely popular up till the end of the 19th century and there were two death knells for them. One was the introduction of cinema, and the other the First World War. So many of the young lads who did the carving and the operating had to go and fight, so family groups lost a lot of their members.

We bought them from the donor on the agreement that we would operate them. We've done two productions: we did *Maria Marten or The Murder in the Red Barn* and we did another one called *The Floating Beacon*. They were hugely appreciated, even at the end of the 20th century.

It is rare to see a 19th-century performer. Any other 19th-century performer – Ellen Terry or Henry Irving – would be in the state the puppet is now! So we can't see Ellen Terry, but we can see these performers, which when you think about it is pretty remarkable.

WAVE MACHINE

Whipple Museum of the History of Science, Cambridge

UP FREE SCHOOL LANE, a tiny street in the centre of Cambridge, is the university's Department of History and Philosophy of Science. The Whipple Museum is inside, up a narrow staircase running past function rooms and boards displaying students' exam results.

Its main room is dominated by a ten foot long Herschel telescope – one of five which George III asked the pioneering astronomer to make in the 1780s. Among an assortment of other objects are glass models of disease-causing fungi, casts of horses' teeth, astrolabes and botanical teaching aids. A regular thump comes from a replica of an astronomical clock made by Richard of Wallingford, abbot of St Albans Abbey from 1327 to 1336.

The wave machine is a large rather graceless object with dust on its rings, hardly recognisable from its clean, fluid incarnation on the museum's website. The animation there shows how rotating the handle at the bottom pulls strings of various lengths to produce a wave movement of white beads along the top – the circular motion of the handle producing an up and down motion of the beads.

The machine was developed in the early 19th century by Baden Powell, Savilian Professor of Geometry at Oxford, to demonstrate the propagation of light waves. 'A glance at an illustration of this kind enables the mind to grasp the idea at once,' he said, 'even when unaccustomed to the mathematical analysis of it.'

Mechanical action was regarded as the most fundamental and therefore the most desirable framework for scientific explanation at the time. Devices such as the wave machine may have been developed to help the constructor clarify theories to themselves. Later in the century they would also have been used for teaching, as they still are today. A mechanical analogy for unseen natural processes could have a 'deep structural correspondence' with them and be a 'heuristic device for theory development, formulation of equations and even suggest the existence of undetected phenomena,' according to Chris Haley, who looked at the wave machine as part of his doctorate in History and Philosophy of Science.

Haley is now head of new technology and start-up research at Nesta, a British charity which promotes innovation. He spoke about the machine's place in the development of scientific thought in the 19th century and about its value today.

> The wave machine caught my attention because from the Physics side I was interested in light and electromagnetism; and then from the History and Philosophy of Science side I was interested in ways of representation, and also in issues of pedagogy and teaching.
>
> Light was one of the big puzzles of 19th-century science. At the start of the century, Thomas Young demonstrated that light could produce interference patterns (the famous 'double slit' experiment which many of us are still taught in school). This showed that light was a wave or vibration. By logical extension, the argument went, it must have been a wave within something – a medium which was to light as air is to sound. An enormous amount of intellectual effort was spent on understanding this medium, known as the aether, and how the properties of light might arise from different kinds of vibration within it.
>
> The dominant mode of explanation in the early 19th century – the fundamental way of understanding anything – was mechanical. The chief proponent of this was William Thomson, Baron Kelvin, who complained about the 'aphasia' of mathematical formulae, and said:

'I never satisfy myself until I can make a mechanical model of a thing. If I can make a mechanical model I can understand it. As long as I cannot make a mechanical model all the way through I cannot understand; and that is why I cannot get the electromagnetic theory.'

The electromagnetic theory to which Kelvin referred was one of the major scientific achievements of the 19th century: James Clark Maxwell's discovery that the medium which transferred light was the same medium which transferred electromagnetic waves. And from there it's a short step to saying light was an electromagnetic wave.

Powell's machine fits within this context, and was intended to help understand the phenomenon of polarisation. Our theory of polarisation hasn't changed a great deal since the late 19th century. Polarisation means the orientation in which light, as a wave, oscillates. What Powell's wave machine shows us is how you can take circularly-polarised light and change this into linearly-polarised light. By manipulating a simple control on the machine you can make a spiral oscillation compress into a flat, polarised oscillation.

But what the electromagnetic theory meant for scientists and physicists (terms both coined in the first half of the 19th century) was that models of light then had to incorporate not just optical phenomena but electromagnetic effects too. Models became progressively more complicated until they reached a point where they broke down because they were trying to incorporate too many complex phenomena.

What we see, then, is a change in thinking from the middle of the 19th century, where you had people like Kelvin quite wedded to mechanical explanation; through people like

Maxwell who used mechanical models but really as a scaffolding to make something different; finally followed by people like Hertz, who wrote 'Maxwell's theory is Maxwell's equations'. What Hertz meant by that is 'we don't need these mechanical models as scaffolding, we've got these equations which have great predictive power, let's not worry about how we got there, let's just use the equations.' And that's really quite a crucial turning point in physics and science in general.

There's a great quote from physicist Richard Feynman, writing nearly a century after Maxwell, saying:

'Today we understand better what counts are the equations themselves, not the models used to get them. We can only question whether the equations are true or false; that is answered by doing experiments and untold numbers of experiments have confirmed Maxwell's equations. If we take away the scaffolding used to build it we find that Maxwell's beautiful edifice stands on its own.'

That's important for physics because until you get the rejection of mechanical models you can't free science to develop theories like quantum theory. For quantum theory, we've now got a brilliant theoretical model but only limited interpretations of that – in other words, the equations work amazingly well in generating predictions, despite the fact there is still not consensus as to what exactly the terms of those equations mean in the real world. That's only been permissible because we went through the process with light of trying to develop a mechanical model and then rejecting that – ending up at the point where we accept mathematics as the more fundamental type of explanation. And that was quite a difficult metaphysical journey.

The wave machine is still useful. If you were a young student and wanted to understand what polarised light is, I think it's still able to do that. I can remember learning physics at school and as an undergraduate where we were taught phenomena of waves using pretty similar devices. Of course, it has also gained secondary meaning, so it is now a historical object which can tell us something about 19th-century science and teaching.

I think many of us on a psychological level feel mechanical models are satisfactory because we solve mechanical problems on a daily basis. We use levers, we use handles to open doors and we have a certain intuitive understanding of mechanics, and that was what Kelvin didn't want to lose. It's an interesting question whether mechanics is really more fundamental in its explanation than maths – but I see it as a philosophical rather than a scientific question.

Have we lost anything by moving to mathematical models? It probably depends on what individuals' minds are more attuned to. It changes for different age groups as well. I'm thinking in particular about young children; I have a four-year-old who may have a shaky grasp of maths but a fairly intuitive grasp of some mechanical phenomena. So you would probably choose a different lens and framework to explain a problem to them. And there are other modes of explanation that have gone in or out of fashion. Occasionally chemical metaphors crop up – people talk about crystallisation and distillation of a point and so on.

Does it matter that visitors can't move the machine? Partly; it would obviously be preferable for people to be able to explore an object with all of their senses, but museum curators have this conflict between making objects accessible and preserving them. Preservation is important not least because theories change, analytical techniques change, we want to preserve things for future generations of scholars to come back and reinterpret things.

I think the curious process of putting it in a case and attaching a label does make people look at things differently, though. People often look at it a bit more reverently and sometimes this can be unhelpful because the interpretation may be viewed as the only one possible. Often it's more informed, but it's not the only one.

BRANTLY B2B HELICOPTER

The Helicopter Museum, Weston-super-Mare

IN A HUGE HANGAR off a roundabout on the outskirts of Weston-super-Mare, an American propaganda film from the Vietnam War is playing. Flames shoot up from little huts by palm trees on water as a voice explains that Vietnam is a country 'which does not allow orthodox ground mobility'. It continues, against stirring background music: 'the technology of the free world is pitted against a Communist guerrilla army. The jungles are filled with the sound of an important new weapon in the arsenal of the free world – the sound of the helicopter, the Huey, destroying the links on the Ho Chi Minh trail which connect the guerrillas with their supply lines in North Vietnam.'

This hangar is the Helicopter Museum, which shares a gravelly expanse rather grandly called the Weston Business Park with Cash and Carry Carpets and the Accelerate Motoring School. Nearby is a river and grazing cows; a ridge of the Mendips shimmers in the heat further off.

The museum stands on the former site of the helicopter manufacturing company Westland, now merged with Italian company Agusta and based in nearby Yeovil. Many will know it primarily from the political storm in 1985 and 1986 when Defence Secretary Michael Heseltine resigned over the government's failure to help it resist being bought by the US company Sikorsky.

The museum has inherited many of the company's helicopters, and a huge red cockpit of a Westland Wessex 1969 dominates the view on entering. An Olympic airlines helicopter with a picture of Hermes on the side is so big it looks like an aeroplane. Many are cut open to show the controls. Some are smaller and more friendly-looking, like the Bell 47H-1. Labels are long and detailed; I learn about the co-axial contra-rotating blades on the Kamov Ka-26 from pre-unification East Germany, which enable it to hover for long periods and carry strong loads. The machines resemble giant insects, with their huge convex windscreens like close-ups of flies' eyes, and their skeletal back ends like grasshoppers or mosquitoes.

The Vietnam propaganda film plays next to the museum's Bell UH-1H Iroquois, or Huey, probably used during the 1968 Tet offensive, the Vietcong's programme of surprise attacks. Inside the helicopter, helmets and combat gear are spread out, including a 'mad dog trophy' for crew chief Steve Watts. The Huey was also used in Saudi Arabia by Allied forces during the Gulf War. Connections with events like the Vietnam War and 'the Westland affair' link the machines with the outside world, tempering the impression transport museums sometimes give of a trainspotters' paradise or place for 'boys with toys'.

Museum trustee Elfan Ap Rees, wearing a captain's stripes, guides me to the conservation workshop at the back of the museum to show me the only helicopter which flies (insurance costs are prohibitive for the others). He explains how he became interested in helicopters and why the museum exists.

> The airfield here at Weston-super-Mare was opened before the war as a civil airfield and became an aircraft manufacturing facility during the war. After the war the Bristol Aeroplane Company switched to making helicopters here in the early Fifties, and that carried on until 2002, and that's why Weston has a helicopter museum.
>
> It's the world's biggest helicopter collection – we have 80-85 of them, and quite a few are the only examples in the world left. We have a very strong Russian collection as well as American helicopters from the Vietnam period and since then. We have the world's fastest helicopter, a Westland Lynx.
>
> It's difficult to say how my fascination with helicopters started. I sometimes think it's standing outside Latin lessons because I had been misbehaving, and watching them fly over. I started in the helicopter factory here working on maintenance manuals. But I never saw helicopters there so I ran away and became a pilot for the Fleet Air Arm. In 1977 I started a helicopter magazine which eventually took over and I resigned from my job. Now I publish three helicopter magazines and the museum continues to be a hobby. My fundamental job with the museum is finding helicopter specimens and twisting people's arms to get them here as quickly as possible. I'm chairman of the trustees and volunteer at weekends. The engineering side is done by 50 or 60 volunteers and about 20 either in the archives or the shop.
>
> This Brantly is a two seater with a piston engine, built in Oklahoma in 1966. I try to fly it for three or four hours at

least once a week. It costs about £5000 a year to maintain, but it's worth it to be able to fly and get away from things. This one belongs to me but it's on display in the museum when I'm not flying. The blades are double jointed, so it's a smoother ride than most helicopters. It has a low centre of gravity so it's less likely to tip over when you land.

They are a lot safer than people think they are. For the lay person it's different from flying in a plane because you have such great visibility, a huge panoramic view and you can land just about anywhere.

People think it's difficult to fly helicopters but it's no harder than driving a car. However, in a car you can afford to make mistakes – in a helicopter you can't. So my golden rule is if you had a row with the wife, or you're stressed up, don't fly.

The Verbal

THE WRITTEN WORD SUFFERS IN MUSEUMS. Why are labels so short, so factual, so...dull? In reply, curators would say that objects need priority in display areas. One can read about the exhibits anywhere, look at them only here. A 'book on the wall' is not a good thing and labels – often limited to 50 or 60 words – are for reliable facts about the exhibit, sometimes the result of lengthy research. Longer interpretation can be kept for guided tours, audioguides, or webpages.

But unpredictable things can happen when words are put with objects or images. John Berger's demonstration of this in his 1972 book *Ways of Seeing* is still the most vivid I know. He asks the reader to look at a reproduction of a painting of a cornfield with birds. On the next page is the same picture, but with the caption 'This is the last picture that Van Gogh painted before he killed himself.' Berger comments: 'it is hard to define exactly how the words have changed the image but undoubtedly they have. The image now illustrates the sentence.' Similarly, words have the power to turn objects into illustrations of text, which in gallery spaces is to be avoided.

What makes a good label, and how visitors read them, is something that museums have puzzled over for decades. One curator interviewed for this book said frustratedly that he thought the only part of longer text panels which people read was the information at eye level. This question has been investigated. In research into 'label reading behaviour' in 1987, museum education expert Paulette McManus recorded and studied conversations between 167 groups of visitors to four separate parts of the Natural History Museum. She found that only about half of the conversing groups looked as if they were reading labels, but actually seven in 10 of their conversation transcripts included extracts or paraphrases of them. So about 70% of the groups' conversations included label content, although it did not always look as if they did. However, she thought it unlikely that the entire text would be read, since visitors wouldn't want the label to dominate the conversation.

But research shows that labels are less likely to be remembered than objects. In a study of 81 psychology undergraduates from Jacksonville State University in Florida who visited five natural history exhibitions at the Anniston Museum of Natural History in 1994, Bitgood and Cleghorn found that in all five exhibitions it was the objects themselves that were most clearly remembered. This was followed (in three exhibitions) by sensory elements such as temperature, light and touch and (in two exhibitions) by label content. They commented that visitors' memories of labels was often 'quite idiosyncratic', with only small portions of their content being recalled, often inaccurately.

Museums have also moved away from overly academic 'curator-speak' on labels, with one educator I spoke to saying she wrote label text with 'an intelligent 12-year-old' in mind. Museum educators recommend using provocative headlines, questions, humour, and challenging statements. 'Which is the odd one out?' 'Do you think this is a plant or animal?' but nevertheless writing in this style rarely appears in most labels, at least for adults. However, with the advent of smartphones and Wi-Fi in museums visitors can now create their own interpretation, helped along by technology such as QR codes. Some researchers are even looking into the way that technology can personalise labels for each individual visitor.

In this section are three objects which are made of words, and therefore in one sense need no label. The first is a book. John Milton escaped the plague in 1665 by going to the Buckinghamshire village of Chalfont St Giles, and a copy of *Paradise Lost*, which he probably worked on there, lies open under the low ceilings and centuries-old brickwork of the cottage he lived in.

The second object is outside the Museum of London, currently marooned on a roundabout in the City of London near the Gherkin, the Barbican Centre, and building works for Crossrail. However, Anglican priest John Wesley's description of how his heart was 'strangely warmed' at a religious meeting close by appear on a monument at the entrance, linking the museum with the city's older roads and striking a quieter, more intimate note. We join modern-day Methodists on their yearly pilgrimage to the sculpture.

The third object is the 1827 will of eminent Liverpudlian Thomas Leyland, matter-of-factly sharing out the profits of slaving voyages. The International Museum of Slavery uses it as a reminder of the origin of some of the city's prosperity, which came through the docks where the museum now stands.

PARADISE LOST

Milton's Cottage, Chalfont St Giles

MILTON'S COTTAGE is a low brick building covered in creeper in the Berkshire village of Chalfont St Giles, approached along hilly country lanes in this affluent area west of London. The poet moved here in 1665 to escape the plague and it is likely that he worked on his Biblical epic *Paradise Lost* in the 'pretty box', as his rescuer

Thomas Ellwood called it. Ellwood was put in prison for Quaker activity soon after finding the house for Milton, so could not help him settle in.

Milton had been a member of Oliver Cromwell's government, helping to write its foreign correspondence and propaganda. However, he had survived the Restoration and by this time his writing was less explicitly political.

Inside, writing by or about Milton is everywhere. There is a copy of Charles II's proclamation calling in two of his pro-republican works, *The Defence of the English People* and *Eikonoklastes*, which defended the beheading of Charles I. His sonnet *On His Blindness* appears on a Poems on the Underground poster. In the study six editions of *Paradise Lost* lie like golden tablets under the low beams. There is also an early draft which Milton wrote at Cambridge University, working out his ideas in the form of a five-act drama. Elsewhere are translations – *El Paradis Perdut, Kadotettu paratiisi, Coll Gwynfa*. A Serbo-Croat version was translated by Yugoslav communist dissident Milovan Djilas while he was in prison for publishing statements criticising the post-war Communist regime in the Soviet Union and Eastern Europe.

Curator Edward Dawson describes himself as a 'privileged messenger'. He retired recently after 20 years spent indefatigably and passionately telling tourists, scholars and schoolchildren about the house and about Milton's influence on Britain's language, law and literature. He offered his personal vision of Milton and of his work:

> His self-discipline and photographic memory were quite extraordinary. Getting up at four o'clock in the morning, blind from the age of 44 so the pen was useless, and composing 40 or 50 lines from dawn in his mind, ready for dictation to the amanuensis who would have reported for work, as it were, at about 11 o'clock. And in the cottage here in the country it was his intelligent and supportive

third wife, Betty Minshull, assisted with nice copying from Deborah his 17-year-old daughter by his first wife, who was here with her stepmother escaping the London plague.

He affects us on such subjects as marriage and divorce; his views on non-compatibility were written into the divorce laws throughout the Western world although they were rejected during his lifetime. He helped to plant the seeds of today's democratic mother House of Parliament. He worked as an early form of Foreign Secretary in the next-door office to the founder of the democratic mother house, Oliver Cromwell.

Milton is central to literacy standards. Any good English teacher at sixth form level will tell you just how he stretches their pupils – the wonderful vocabulary of Milton, he's the greatest coiner of words in the Oxford dictionary; his neologism is supreme. Mr Shakespeare is in fourth place behind him in the pecking order. We use him every day and they are commonplace words in the dictionary.

Cambridge University library have all the five or six hundred. You've got echoing, gloom, impassive, rumoured, liturgical, debauchery, dismissive, embellishing, lovelorn, irksome, besotted, self-esteem, didactic, sensuous, pandemonium of course, padlock, terrific, fragrance, complacency, outer space, arch fiend, etc. That's just to whet your appetite! Take 'all hell broke loose'; it's on everyone's tongue on a daily basis. Likewise, very few people know that 'every cloud has a silver lining' is Milton – and there's plenty more where that came from.

You never stop finding out new things. You can arrive here one day and you're brushing up one of his prose works and you find as I did last season that Milton in his

Ready and Easy Way to Establish a Commonwealth was busy making a very erudite case to the Parliament for decentralisation of government by county, so you can say that he was one of the first to outline the devolving of government locally.

Why see the house? Because we have the collection and the evidence that supports the man's genius. The house has all of the first editions of *Paradise Lost* from the 17th century (more than the Bodleian and the British Library), including a first edition which can be seen by appointment. There are also other rare and unique items which support our claim to have the most significant Miltonic bibliography in the world. Evidence in the shape of the volumes, the documents and manuscripts that prove what would otherwise be a totally disbelievable life, a life which has inspired so many people – even Danny Boyle opened the Olympic Games tableau with John Milton.

But I wondered how much the cottage itself told us about the poet. This is Milton's only remaining house, and an atypical one – he was really a Londoner, born in Cheapside, buried in St Giles Cripplegate (now in the Barbican). He only lived here for eight or nine months before returning to the capital, where he stayed for the remaining nine years of his life. So much of what he thought and wrote was a part of the politics of his day, and of the business of Parliament. The cottage is not like Down House, where Darwin did his experiments on earthworms and orchids. Nor is it like Dove Cottage, set in the landscape which inspired Wordsworth's poetry. In fact, I found it somewhat gloomy, a shrine constructed after the event. After the event for Milton, because he was no longer in the thick of politics when he lived here; for us, because it was Britain's only pro-republican revolution and poetry was part of politics, which is not true now.

But in an inspired move by the curators, a large hardback copy of *Paradise Lost* lies open on a table in the centre of the study, a pulled-up chair and white gloves inviting the visitor to turn the pages and read. It is a luxuriously produced Folio Society edition, large text with generous margins, illustrated by Milton's great admirer William Blake. Blake's serpent traps and caresses Eve, thick coils wrapped around her whole body. It gently prods the fruit into her mouth with its own. I open it at random and come across Satan's speech in Book IV, in which he swears enmity to God:

> So farewell, hope; and with hope farewell, fear;
> Farewell, remorse! all good to me is lost;
> Evil, be thou my good; by thee at least
> Divided empire with Heaven's King I hold,
> By thee, and more than half perhaps will reign;
> As Man ere long, and this new world, shall know.

Milton's verse always pushes onwards. Rhythmic and flowing at the same time, the words immediately enliven the house, momentarily making a mini-theatre of the room where Milton and his wife Betty sat too.

WESLEY MONUMENT

Museum of London

'IN THE EVENING I went very unwillingly to a society in Aldersgate Street, where one was reading Luther's preface to the Epistle to the Romans. About a quarter before nine, while the leader was describing the change which God works in the heart thro' faith in

Christ, I felt my heart strangely warm'd. I felt I did trust in Christ alone for salvation: and an assurance was given me that He had taken away my sins, even mine, and saved me from the law of sin and death.'

This statement, barely legible on a dark grey monument outside the Museum of London, stopped me in my tracks when I first saw and read it. It was half familiar to me, and it seemed both unexpected and very appropriate to have outside the museum – much better, say, than a generalisation about the city such as Samuel Johnson's well-worn comment, now a cliché, 'When a man is tired of London, he is tired of life', which, anyway, isn't true. Wesley's record of a private, intense experience in a nearby street struck me as an appropriate link between the museum and its locale. It also seemed quite a random choice and so a good accompaniment to the fragments of evidence and experience from passing centuries which are found inside, often chance survivals or discoveries. I also found it charming that Wesley mixed the large abstractions of 'faith' and 'salvation' with everyday details, in Aldersgate Street about a quarter to nine.

It has never had the same impact for me since, and it turned out that the monument in fact has much more to do with the Methodist Church, which Wesley is credited with founding, than with the museum. It was put up in 1988, the 250th anniversary of Wesley's 'heartwarming moment', and is cared for by the Methodists' 'Aldersgate committee'. Methodists make a pilgrimage to it on the 24th of May each year, the date of Wesley's experience, also calling at the grave of Wesley's mother Susannah, at St Paul's Cathedral, and Wesley's Chapel, which Wesley built and where he is buried. The monument will remain after the museum's move to the site of the old Smithfield market, which it plans to make by 2021.

These Methodist pilgrims have a short service at the monument, which I watched in 2014 when about 70 people attended. A scooter session on a ramp in the forecourt had just finished, the sun came out after a shower, and raindrops glistened on the monument. A minister jumped up and stood on a low wall in front of it to do the reading. Hymns were sung, a prayer said and a wreath laid.

The congregation included a choir from the Ghana-based Susannah Wesley Mission Auxiliary (SUWMA). Images of Susannah Wesley were printed on their purple and white dresses and headdresses, along with pictures of a Mrs Agnes Afriye Amankwa, one of the founding members of the organisation.

Among the group was the Reverend Jennifer Potter, a minister at Wesley's Chapel in City Road. She worked as a missionary and teacher in Zambia and Botswana for over 20 years before coming to London in 1996 and being ordained in 2004. Earlier she had given me her views on the monument and on the importance of Wesley's conversion to Methodists.

> I like the idea of the monument, that those significant words from Wesley's journal for May 24th are written on a large flame – representing the work of the Holy Spirit. If you look on Aldersgate Street just north of the big roundabout you will see a smaller plaque which marks, as far as is known, the actual site of the meeting place where John Wesley went on the evening of 24th May and heard the reading which had such an impact on him.
>
> Opinion differs on the significance of the 'heartwarming' moment. What is undisputed is that after 24th May (and the 21st May when John Wesley's brother Charles had a similar experience which is marked by a plaque in Little Britain nearby) the Wesleys began preaching with much greater conviction and started to travel around more and set up 'societies' – groups of Christians attracted by their message. John and Charles were Anglican priests and did not intend to set up a new church – rather they hoped to invigorate the Anglican Church.

Wesley himself did not make a great deal of his May 24th experience in subsequent years or at least he did not write about it and, as far as we know, no commemorations were held in his lifetime – he was too busy doing new things to think of revisiting the past. But the conviction of God's grace for all people – 'prevenient grace' – God's unconditional love, was at the heart of their preaching. But this was not unique to Methodists – for example, the Moravians also emphasised this and contributed to the Wesleys' 'conversion' experiences.

This part of London is an important place of pilgrimage for Methodists and other Christians, and the monument is part of that.

THOMAS LEYLAND'S WILL

International Slavery Museum, Liverpool

LIVERPOOL'S ALBERT DOCK is quiet on this cloudy afternoon; a few people chat in each wine bar and a Japanese tourist takes a picture of the Beatles made of sweets in the window of Quay Confectionery (established 1988).

Inside Merseyside Maritime Museum screams, bangs, creaks and raised voices come from the third floor, which houses the International Slavery Museum. A film shows Solomon, a slave on the run, who is panicked and breathing heavily. A voice tells the end of the story: 'The master's hounds got him.' Another display is about 'branding a negress'.

Liverpool outdid Bristol and London in this 'melancholy traffic', claimed Bristol-based anti-slavery resident William Matthews in a 1794 business directory he published. 'The people of Liverpool, in their indiscriminate rage for Commerce and for getting money at all events have nearly engrossed this Trade,' he said. The city did dominate the trade; between 1741 and 1750, 43 per cent of the ships involved in the British slave trade departed from the Liverpool docks and between 1801 and 1807, when slavery was abolished in the UK, Liverpool accounted for 79 per cent.

Merseyside shipping and dock growth in the 18th century fuelled this, combined with rapid industrialisation after 1750 and a rising population available for factory work, whose products could be exported to Africa. The city also gained from safe shipping routes around the north of Ireland and smuggling channels through the Isle of Man until 1765. Liverpool merchants were good at building effective business partnerships along the West African coast, especially in the Bight of Biafra where many slaves were put onto British ships, and at managing payment procedures with Caribbean agents and London sugar commission houses. Liverpool merchants also quickly capitalised on new markets such as islands ceded to Britain by France after 1763 including Grenada, Tobago, St. Vincent and Dominica; and Cuba, Demerara and Trinidad later in the century. In all, Liverpool ships delivered over 1.1 million slaves to the New World.

The galleries map the triangular slave trade, as well as exploring life in West Africa and legacies of slavery. They show how ships went from Britain to West Africa with goods such as textiles and shells, exchanged these with traders in Africa for slaves which they transported over the Atlantic to the Caribbean, then exchanged them there for sugar and other crops before sailing back to Britain. I read British surgeon Alexander Falconbridge's comment on conditions on the Atlantic voyages in his 1788 book *An Account of the Slave Trade on the Coast of Africa*: 'The deck that is the floor of their rooms was so covered with blood and mucus which had preceded from them in consequence of the flux that it resembled a slaughterhouse. It is not in the power of human imagination to picture itself a situation so dreadful and disgusting.'

Perhaps because of the gallery's relentless message and overpowering multimedia, I find myself drawn instead to the objects with little or no interpretation. One of these is a beautiful large teardrop-shaped carved stone, broken at the tip, one of the few objects which survive from the Caribbean's original people. It was made by the Taino people, who lived mainly on Hispaniola (now Haiti and the Dominican Republic) and parts of Cuba and Puerto Rico. The Tainos were wiped out by the slavery and disease brought by Spanish colonisers. As I look at the stone's smooth lines it seems to escape for a moment from the matrix of interpretation around it.

Another object left mainly to speak for itself is a Christmas photo of the staff of the African Oil Nuts Company and Miller Brothers at Badagry in Nigeria in 1923. Twenty black men, naked from the waist up, stand in rows like a school class. Each has one letter or number of '1923 Badagry Merry Xmas.' painted in white on their chest. The few white people sitting at the front are fully clothed and have no letters painted on them.

In 1776, Thomas Leyland was working for an Irish merchant, Gerald Dillon, with whom he won a £20,000 lottery prize. He used his share to start trading in commodities including slaves, initially in partnership with other local merchants. The profit on one voyage made by Leyland's slave ship 'Lottery' in 1798 was more than £12,000 (more than £900,000 today). Records from the journey made by his ship 'Hannah' contain instructions to the captain to treat his crew with humanity and to show the 'utmost tenderness to the Negroes'. The museum's evidence about slaving voyages suggests it is unlikely this happened.

The museum also gives accounts for 294 slaves sold at Kingston, Jamaica, with details on the purchasers and prices. It categorises slaves into types: privileged men, privileged women, cargo men, cargo women, men boys, women girls, boys, and girls. Altogether, Leyland had an interest in at least 69 slave voyages.

In 1802, Leyland purchased the estate of Walton Hall north of Liverpool and established a bank – Leyland & Bullins – in partnership with his nephew, who was also involved in the slave trade. This was taken over by Midland Bank in 1908, which was later absorbed by HSBC. Leyland was mayor three times between 1798 and 1820; in fact, all of Liverpool's 20 lord mayors who held office between 1787 and 1807 were involved in the slave trade. When he died in 1827, he was one of the richest men in Britain.

Leyland's will is in a drawer, a bundle of yellow parchment – not displayed so that it can be read – marked with a bulky seal. It is used as evidence of profit made from a cruel and inhumane trade. I spoke to education demonstrator Mitty Ramachandran about the will and about the work of the museum.

> The will is not an object we use directly in our handling sessions. Sometimes it can be difficult to engage students with the subject of slavery, so we have some objects which aren't particularly nice. Shackles and neck irons, branding irons and things like that – although of course, we use replicas. It is a way of getting hands-on with these objects. Rather than having to read volumes of text, if they've got objects in front of them sometimes it makes it more real. But we do ask people not to try objects like that on, as a sign of respect.
>
> We do use texts; mainly first-hand accounts – the African perspective and the voice of the enslaved. We are trying to make that link between Liverpool and transatlantic slavery very obvious. I don't know how leading it is but we are a campaigning museum so we don't shy away from that sort of thing.

I think it's exceptionally important to know that Liverpool benefited from slavery – people need to be aware of that to have knowledge of the history of Liverpool. We still have physical reminders of that like the Town Hall, streets named after slave traders such as Earl Street, Tarleton Street, Penny Lane (arguably named after James Penny, though I think that one's disputed). These are physical reminders that you can't get away from. It's not just coincidence that the museum is on the Albert Dock; it was close to where the action was happening and where ships were being fixed and sent to West Africa with goods.

We think of Britain being wealthy, but that wealth was built on the backs of other people. Those myths and ideas surrounding race that were perpetuated by transatlantic slavery still persist. So if you have 400 years of people thinking in a particular way, even if laws have changed those attitudes do not change overnight. And if we are still living with them we need to understand how and why those attitudes came about.

The Domestic

IN ELIZABETH BISHOP'S POEM *Crusoe in England*, Robinson Crusoe arrives back home after his years spent alone on an island. He looks at his knife, whose surfaces, colours and imperfections he knows so intimately, and realises sorrowfully that it has changed; its 'living soul' has now gone. The local museum has asked if they can have his possessions, he says, and he cannot understand why anyone would want to.

How indeed can museums want things whose significance lies in their relationship with their owners? What meaning can they have for others? Sometimes the museum may actually decide that the owner, if he or she is well-known like Robinson Crusoe, is important. But more often domestic objects are made to tell other, wider stories – of an era, perhaps, or a particular technology or a place.

The first two objects here each have a personal and a more general story mixed. The first, a toy farm set, was an imaginary world for a little girl and for the museum shows how city dwellers viewed the countryside. The second, a plate, was initially a cheap acquisition for a woman setting up home. Now, as a design historian, she understands it as part of a history of ceramics and as something which helps her to understand how gifts forge links between people. The third, a tiny table, is valued solely because of its original owner, Jane Austen, and its place in her writing life and her home.

BRITAINS TOY FARM SET

Museum of English Rural Life, Reading

INSIDE A PLASTIC BUBBLE attached to the wall in the Museum of English Rural Life is an idyllic miniature farm. A farmer sits in a tractor next to a dovecote; clean pigs, horses and chickens cluster among trees and fences. Larger exhibits loom nearby – an Arts and Crafts sideboard, a Glastonbury festival poster, rows of ploughs, and a horse gin: a pole which a horse would pull in circles to turn a mill wheel. This toy farm has 361 lead and plastic pieces, including farmworkers, cows, sheep, fences and hedges. Toys such as this started becoming very popular after World War I, as people rejected war games and toy soldiers.

The museum likes tiny objects since traditional farm equipment, such as combine harvesters, is too large and often too expensive to store and display. Assistant curator Ollie Douglas says it is now 'addressing the late 20th century in the miniature rather than the massive'. It is also collecting representations of the countryside in images, books or films, since this is how many city dwellers in Reading and beyond will know it.

Philippa Hughes, a retired woman who lives in Reading, was given the set when she was six or seven and played with it for the next eight or nine years. She donated it to the museum and told me what it meant to her as a child.

> I was very lucky – my mother was very tolerant, and I had the farm permanently out on half my bedroom floor, which was only old lino. I painted streams and made fields so I had a complete farm there the whole time.
>
> I did the milking, I brought the harvest in. I made ploughed fields out of corrugated cardboard, so I had the furrows already there! I always liked using the horses – I made miniature harnesses for all the carthorses out of fuse wire and leather strips. For the milking machines I used plastic bottle tops and plastic from the covering on electric wiring. In a way it wasn't really a game, I just did a daily routine. Neither of my parents were in rural life at all, I just always loved it.
>
> My birthday treat was to go to Henley on the bus, picnic by the river, and buy a Britains model from the toy shop in Henley. We went to the cinema occasionally, perhaps twice a year, but most of the time was spent in the garden and the house... plenty of time.
>
> I did almost go into farming - I got an offer from Writtle Agricultural College but didn't take it up.
>
> My children played with it, and then my grandchildren. Every now and then as a special treat, they had it out on the kitchen table. Last time they just got them out and looked and put them all together – they usually don't have

time to do any more than that; they are rushing off to do something else. Children play in different ways now – they don't concentrate for very long on one thing and their lives are so full and busy. We had few toys but we enjoyed them.

I've no sense of loss at all that the toys are going to the museum. Hopefully it will show visitors the different levels and changes in the farming world – such as using horses for ploughing, different styles of tractor. I still think of the farm. I love miniatures, always have done. It's the size and being a complete replica of something big. I have kept one as a reminder – a pony and trap with figures.

'Homemaker' Plate

Brighton Museum and Art Gallery

In the late 1950s and 60s, many people ate their dinners off armchairs – pictures of armchairs, that is. 'Homemaker' plates were decorated with images of sofas, pot plants, carving knives, armchairs – and plates. The V&A rather stiffly calls it an 'amusingly self-referential' design.

During and after World War II ceramics for the home market could only be manufactured in white to save resources, but in 1952 colour was allowed again. A year earlier the Festival of Britain had presented a new wave of stylish products to the public, who were ready to leave wartime austerity behind. Factories began to employ talented young designers and the New Look, at first used to describe

Christian Dior clothes, was applied to other products. The 'Homemaker' design was part of this optimism.

The design was the work of Enid Seeney, who had been the first woman to be trained at the Spode and Copland works before moving to design company Ridgway. She originally called the range 'Furniture'. Woolworth's ordered their first tea sets in May 1957, four months before Seeney left work to start a new married life in Devon. The first she knew about the popularity of the design was when she saw it in Woolworth's in Plymouth.

Homemaker ware was cheap to manufacture. Plates were decorated at the Ridgway factory in Stoke-on-Trent using the new Murray-Curvex machine, which used a gelatine dome to transfer colour from an engraved copper plate onto the unglazed china. The machine did not work with convex surfaces, so for larger pots tissue paper was used to transfer the pattern (the tissue paper had to be cut up, which is why the pattern on the coffee pots and casserole dishes is in pieces). The tissue paper was applied with water to the surface of the china and sealed with a clear glaze. Pieces were then kiln-fired. The cups and the casserole and teapot lids are plain black, which stylishly complements the pattern.

Woolworth's piled Homemaker kitchenware high and sold it cheap. Teapots went for 10 to 15 shillings (50-75p) and teacups for 2/6 (12 ½p); a full set of plates, bowls and cups cost 31 shillings (£1.55). Many of the families who bought the range could not have afforded the more upmarket furniture shown on it, such as the chic kidney-shaped table. Indeed, the design helped to give the shop's image a boost: 'Smart, stylish and modern,' said an advert of the time. 'Can it be Woolworth?'

The line has since become highly collectable; a 40-piece set went for just over £400 at Bonhams in 2010. 'I just love the black and white vintage furniture icons, the simple rounded shape of the items and their overall durability,' says collector and gardening blogger Gillian Carson. 'I have scoured the charity shops for even one plate from this sacred range, but have had to resort to eBay to get my hands on one for my kitchen wall,' says Claire Smyth, who blogs about 'retro wonders'. 'A red sandwich plate has been found in Australia,' writes Simon Moss in *Homemaker: A 1950s Design Classic*, which tells the history of the design and tracks different versions. There is even a reworked 2014 version by Eyal Burstein for 1882 Ltd, in partnership with Vivienne Westwood, featuring a pile of books and 21st-century furniture.

A Homemaker plate sits in Brighton Museum and Art Gallery, housed in the Royal Pavilion, George IV's nutty Orient-themed pleasure palace. Across the road is Brighton University's History of Art and Design department. Louise Purbrick, senior lecturer in the department, sets a place for the 'Homemaker' plate in design history and in her own life and thought.

> This has a black-and-white pattern with what we would now call kitsch objects, I would say, all around the rim and in the middle. These are 1950s objects, which I know partly on sight and partly because of my training as a design historian. I'm not sure that other people would definitely say '1950s' though. In the centre is this curvy coffee table which people might think of as 70s, actually; it has that sense of being a little bit funky; a bit space age.
>
> The reason I know this plate is because I had one. I was a punk – a little bit of a young punk, and in the 1980s I was setting up home – or at least, I was moving into a flat – and I bought a few of these in second-hand shops in Worthing.
>
> Mine was a tea plate. They would have been ever so cheap – 20p each, perhaps less. I really liked them, but you change your mind about things or you feel you can't carry them, you don't know where you're going and you might

be moving from an unfurnished to a furnished place so I got rid of them. And then I came across it in the 20th-century gallery in the V&A and thought 'why did I not keep those?' But when I bought it I had no idea I was going to be an art and design historian; I was working as a home help; thinking about doing social history; I was retaking 'A' levels and didn't go to university (that is, to a polytechnic) until I was 23.

The V&A started to collect modern and everyday ceramics in the 1980s – it was a big shift in their collecting policy. I can understand why they chose this plate because it's a very good example of English modernism. It's not the kind of modernism of Bauhaus, but it's got something of that about it. And the other important thing is that it's a female designer, Enid Seeney, and women in the ceramics industry is an important topic for design historians.

China is also very important in the work I have done on wedding presents using the Mass Observation Archive, records of everyday life, at Sussex University. There are some objects, like dinner or tea services, which people keep and rarely or never use. And that's a really interesting category of things. And this led me into thinking about gifts. What separates a gift from the everyday things that we use and throw away?

So I read anthropologists, particularly Marcel Mauss and his notion of a gift that is obligatory and reciprocal. A gift has to be returned; it's not free – it binds you into a relationship with someone. And what happens at weddings is that people have to give, and even though those gifts are not returned, you do return a transaction which may be an invitation to dinner, an arrangement to remain part of that community or to give a present to their children when they get married. So a gift helps to sustain relationships. The objects on the plate are a bit like a wedding collection actually.

And wedding presents often stand for the giver; so people would say things like 'I had this lovely tea service that my aunt gave me and I rarely use it, but on the occasions we do, we think of her.' So it may help you recall your family line or your social position in that family. When people lose or break china, it can also somehow signify a passing of a life; there's a sense that it can hold together bonds between people across time, because it lasts longer than us. And that's partly why it is kept in cupboards and not used.

The plate has also got quite a humorous and kitsch punk look, like people who liked the B-52s, which I didn't exactly, but I can see how punk in the 1980s would have some of that humour. Kitsch can be thought of as over-decorated and standing for what Pierre Bourdieu would call vulgar, popular taste because it's easy to read; you can see the images on the surface of the kitsch object, whereas fine art would be abstract and you would contemplate its significance and deep meanings. So kitsch would stand for ideas of poor taste or working class taste but also a style that's understandable, translatable, and assimilated into life. But I think kitsch now has become redeemed in the way in which a vintage buyer in Brighton, for example, is able to identify something that is at the margins of good taste and which can be recuperated as a sign of knowledge of what's in and out of fashion.

I wish I still had that plate.

JANE AUSTEN'S WRITING TABLE

Jane Austen's House Museum, Chawton

ENTRY TO JANE AUSTEN'S HOUSE is through the gift shop. This brings home both her extraordinary popularity and the continuing creative responses to her six novels, making it unnecessary for any academic to argue her relevance to the 21st century. DVDs of the many film adaptations line the shelves along with accompanying behind-the-scenes books: interviews with the stars, guides to locations used. Then there is Mr Darcy wrapping paper, a Make Your Own Mr Darcy doll kit and cut out figures of Colin Firth and Jennifer Ehle, who played Darcy and Elizabeth Bennett in the best-known and loved adaptation of *Pride and Prejudice*, the 1995 BBC TV mini-series.

A display on the 'Jane Austen banknote concept' leans against a wall in the next room, since the governor of the Bank of England, Mark Carney, is due at the museum in two weeks to announce that Austen's portrait will appear on the British £10 note. And in case anyone should forget the novels themselves, copies of Mansfield Park are set out on shelves in the garden.

Austen lived here with her sister and mother (both called Cassandra) and their friend Martha Lloyd between 1809 and her death in 1817. The cottage was part of an estate which her brother Edward had inherited, and brought much-needed security to the women after financial uncertainty caused by her father's death in 1805. It was her most productive time as a writer. Here she revised *Sense and Sensibility* and *Pride and Prejudice* for publication, and completed four further novels (*Emma* and *Mansfield Park* were published while she lived here, *Persuasion* and *Northanger Abbey* after her death).

The table which Austen is 'reputed' to have written at, according to the text panel, is in the dining room next to the low window. It is tiny, about mid-thigh height, marked, and has woodworm holes. It is much less grand than the dining table next to it where the women ate their meals. After Austen's death it was given to an elderly servant by her mother.

The table lends itself so well to our image of Austen: the pioneering woman writer with no room of her own sitting in the corner at a second-class piece of furniture, looking out of the window at passing society and drawing inspiration from their habits and foibles. In the first biography of Austen, her nephew Edward Austen-Leigh wrote that his aunt did not want servants or visitors to know what she was doing. 'She wrote upon small sheets of paper, which could easily be put away, or covered with a piece of blotting paper. There was between the front door and the offices, a swing door which creaked when it was opened; but she objected to having this little inconvenience remedied, because it gave her notice when anyone was coming.' My guidebook repeats this anecdote, but it doesn't quite ring true – the table seems too small to hide anything, for one thing. When I mention the story to an attendant, she is also sceptical. Austen biographer Claire Tomalin says the story 'can be only half true', pointing out that Austen could not have hidden a full manuscript under a blotter, and could easily have worked in another room. But Tomalin cannot resist the table, saying elsewhere that it 'speaks to every visitor of the modesty of genius'.

Not least of the responses to Austen's work have been other novels, from *Bridget Jones's Diary*'s degraded and hilarious form of Elizabeth Bennett and her dilemmas, to *The Jane Austen Book Club* by Karen Joy Fowler, which explores the lives and loves of six 21st-century Americans in the town of Davis, California, as they discuss the novels. Another response from the US is Cindy Jones's *My Jane Austen Summer*, whose heroine Lily has 'squeezed herself into undersized relationships all her life, hoping one might grow as large as those found in the Jane Austen novels she loves'. A *Mansfield Park* literary festival in Britain helps her to find herself.

Cindy Jones is a fan of the writing table, and feels the Jane Austen House Museum brings the author to life in a way that other places with Austen links, such as the house where she lived in Bath, do not. She told me why, and describes her fascination with the author.

> Jane Austen's writing table is the most unassuming piece of furniture with the most impressive backstory I've ever met, and seeing it had a powerful effect on me.
>
> After reading The Six, I felt a void. I tried everything: re-reading her novels, reading her contemporaries, and reading the biographies and letters. I joined The Jane Austen Society of North America (JASNA), watched adaptations, and even once dressed in Regency attire. To my amazement, I discovered I was not alone. Janeites from all walks of life and all ends of the world feel the void, and each has their own way of filling it.
>
> The best medicine for me was to write the novel I wanted to read. *My Jane Austen Summer* is the story of a young woman who believes she may have realized her dream of living in a novel when she is invited to a literary festival in England, where actors recreate scenes from *Mansfield Park*. Spending five long years at my writing desk, writing Jane Austen into my fiction, thoroughly filled the void and enabled Jane Austen and I to settle into a more balanced relationship.
>
> When I had almost finished, I went to England with my eleven-year-old son to check some facts and to meet the Jane Austen I'd written into my story. I was nervous, since I'd taken the liberty of writing about our relationship even though we'd never met. In The *Jane Austen Book Club*, Karen Joy Fowler writes that each of us has a private Austen. My private Austen disdains the harlequinization of

her novels, the Darcy craze, and the gathering of people in Regency costume (except as they might all be subject to the sharp end of her pen). On the other hand, my private Austen knows that through writing it is possible to spend a good part of each day living in a novel, presiding over an imaginary world.

But what if I was wrong? Fanny Price would never presume to write first, ask questions later. I could already feel the sharp end of the pen exiling me to Portsmouth. I also ran the risk of discovering I'd based my book on a deep misunderstanding. Five years of my life could go down the drain. Not to mention what my agent would say.

I went to Jane Austen's front door in Gay Street in Bath. She was not there. I visited her crowded museum. She was not there, either. I visited Jane Austen's grave in Winchester Cathedral. Oh, dear.

And then I visited Chawton. Standing in the simple room where the modest writing table occupied a spot near the window, I felt my Jane Austen's presence. Here, at last, was the writer who nailed Aunt Norris and Maria Bertram to the page while everyone else did chores. Seeing the little table in the context of the unassuming cottage and the small village gave me goose-bumps. And understanding that Jane Austen, with almost no formal education and hemmed in by class and gender, produced some of the greatest novels of all time from that humble place moved me.

The Jane Austen I met at the writing table was indeed the person I had imagined: physically present at the table, yet mentally far away, working in a universe of her own creation.

Coal mine
The Big Pit

The Huge

My strongest childhood memory of museums is of looking up at the full-size blue whale replica hanging from the ceiling in the Natural History Museum. As far as I can put that experience into words, it was sheer awe, tinged with fear, that a living thing so large could exist. Such opportunities to examine huge objects from unusual positions is something that museums offer – walking underneath a whale, drinking coffee near a 12-metre-high North American totem pole, peering through dinosaur ribs. Scale is also an aspect of objects which cannot properly be offered in the digital realm.

Huge objects often exert huge power, as the whale did over me as a child. They may be hard to move, change, control; and might have to be shared with others. For museums, very large objects are often difficult to acquire, store, transport and display. And how far does our definition of an 'object' go – can the coal mine in this section really be called an object? What about a shop? A landscape?

Each of the objects that follow had a powerful hold over many people. The mine was a workplace on which local people depended for their livelihoods; the ship was a repository of hope, taking emigrants from Ireland to America; and the Celtic cross bears powerful stories made to engender wonder and obedience in its observers.

Coal Mine

Big Pit National Coal Museum, Blaenavon

BLAENAVON, a town in south-east Wales, owed its prosperity and population growth to the minerals in its rocks; its iron and coal helped to fuel the Industrial Revolution. The Big Pit is one of its mines, and the pithead still rises above the gentle surrounding hills. Ironworks were opened here in 1789, the metal needed for railways and for armaments for Britain's wars with America and with France. The coal mine opened in 1860, supplying coal for rocketing numbers of ships, trains, factories and houses. Demand peaked just before the First World War, with a quarter of a million miners in Welsh coalfields producing 57,000,000 tons in 1913. The coal industry then declined because of the depression of the 20s and 30s and competition from oil.

The Big Pit closed in February 1980 because it was unviable, and opened to visitors three years later. It was thus already a museum by the start of the Conservative government's pit closure programme of 1984-5 in which 29 Welsh collieries were shut down. The area is now a World Heritage Site because of its industrial landscape, and its 30s-style tourist logo shows a burly miner leaning contemplatively on his spade and staring into the sun, a design which also echoes the celebration of workers' muscle in Soviet art. The pit is also used for geological research and tours, since it is unusual to have access to such deep coal measures.

Ten of us gather in a reception room for an underground tour with an ex-miner, John Scandrett. We put on caps, helmets, lamps, belts, batteries and a 'rebreather' which will supply oxygen for an hour if necessary. 'Into the valley of the shadow of death,' jokes Scandrett as we step into the lift. Doors clang and we go down 90 metres in a shaft drilled for iron ore in 1860, changing to coal in

1880. The lift moves at two metres per second. 'When it is working, it goes three times faster,' Scandrett tells us. He fixes a child with his eye. 'Back in Victorian times you would have worked.' He hands round a piece of iron ore, then coal for us to examine, and tells us that women would have pushed trolleys underground.

What follows is a tour of a few places in the mine and snippets of striking and important information about it, often connected with working conditions or technology. We pass round a Davy lamp, invented in 1815, whose flame turns blue when flammable gas is present.

Children used to work with their families until they were 15, and got tokens for coal which could only be spent in shops owned by mine owners. A child would have spent his or her time sitting next to the stalls in the dark; their job was to open doors for horses. 'You've heard the term pitch black – this is pitch black.' Horses pulled coal along the underground railway and lived in the dark for up to 10 years. 'If they survived they were good for next to nothing,' says Scandrett. They were often sent to the slaughterhouse. We see stalls with horses' names – King, Hercules, Goliath, Nancy. In 1930 72 horses were used in the mine. The last two horses were brought to the surface in 1972, after conveyor belts had taken over.

In 1842 the Earl of Shaftesbury's report revealed the shocking conditions in which children as young as five were working in mines. The Mine and Collieries Act of the same year prohibited women and children under ten from working underground. But mining remained a dangerous occupation; for example, in 1865, 27 miners including six boys were killed in an explosion at Bedwellty colliery in Monmouthshire. From 1947, when the mines were nationalised, miners got two weeks' holiday per year. The tour takes us to the late 1960s when the mine was mechanised. The current mine is inspected every four hours to make sure it's safe.

The mine itself is only part of a huge colliery site with a blacksmith's forge, canteen, repair shop and other buildings. There are also the pithead baths, whose installation in 1939 meant that miners no longer had to walk home dirty to sit in fireside tubs or risk pneumonia with an outdoors wash-down, and their wives no longer had to boil huge pots of water for them. Next to it are the miners' dirty and clean lockers – clean lockers to put clothes in on arrival, dirty lockers to take out working clothes, then the reverse process at the end of the shift.

In another part of the mine, a noise and light display reconstructs mechanised mining and introduces a chainsaw-like tool nicknamed 'the widow maker' because of the lung-infesting dust it threw out. Balanced displays touch on equipment, mining unions, the impact of fossil fuels on the environment, different types of energy. There are miners' strike mugs, a policeman's truncheon, a satirical Thatcher figurine. Fittingly, the mining souvenirs 'industry' is covered. A video offers some final words: 'The tale of comradeship is no bad thing to come out of the mucky heart of a big Welsh pit'. 'Comradeship' is perhaps chosen to cover normal work camaraderie and the more political solidarity miners have shown over the decades in response to governments' attempts to change their working conditions or close down pits.

A focus on stories of heroism and technological innovation is not without its critics. 'The industrial heritage initiatives that promise regeneration in these towns perversely promote mining as ultimately ennobling and environmentally benign,' said Gareth Hoskins, lecturer in Human Geography at Aberystwyth University in a piece in *Planet* magazine. He believes that coalmining museums need to highlight the ecological and social damage caused by mines and the wealth inequalities they left behind them. 'Can we draw connections between the 19th-century industrial community of Blaenavon and the contemporary community of Blaenau Gwent where a sense of hopelessness is so prevalent that one in six of the borough's residents is in receipt of prescriptions for anti-depressants?' he asks. He envisages Blaenavon as a place that could foster revolutionary politics, union activity and campaigning against climate change and globalisation.

Perhaps because we are on the actual site of the mine, with an ex-miner, I sense some difference between the selection and presentation of intriguing and shocking stories during the tour, and the more mundane daily activity which might have gone on. When I speak to John Scandrett after the tour I indeed feel that stories of heroism, politics and disasters are part of a presentation of coalmining at the site which coincide only partly with his experience and outlook. He is keen to emphasise the more everyday aspects of mining – joking with colleagues, the ups and downs of work.

Scandrett worked in mining for 27 years, mainly as a deputy – responsible for procedures such as safety inspections and materials supply. He started working at the Blaenavon pit in 1966, left in 1980 when it closed and worked in other pits nearby for the next 12 years. He was a member of NACODS (The National Union of Colliery Overmen, Deputies and Shotfirers), whose members were not part of the year-long strike by the NUM (National Union of Miners) to try to stop the pit closure programme. After leaving mining in 1992 he worked at Tesco before returning to the Big Pit as a guide. He talked to me about his background and experience of mining. What follows is his personal view.

> When I was in school they were having entrance exams for heavy industry – coal, steel, electricity, all sorts of things. I come from a non-mining family but chose mining because it was a job for the future, for life, because it was such an alive industry. I have got no regrets.
>
> The good bit about mining was the camaraderie really; as soon as you start talking to the boys it was like you'd never been away; whereas in an office if you said 'Oh that sweater you've got on – your mother-in-law doesn't like you,' you can't do that. In mining you can. My eldest boy was in the

army for 10 years. When he went into the army he realised what camaraderie was – everybody looked after each other. And it's the same in mining.

The bad part was closure really. And underground you'd have incidents that happen – that would be hard work, like you'd have a roof fall, machinery breaking, so there were difficult parts. It was a very physical job. But when it became closure, closure, closure, I thought 'I've had enough of this'.

So I got out completely and went to work for Tesco for 17 years, in the distribution centre. Twelve years of that was in an office and it became very pressured. You'd be looking at the clock and you'd want the clock to go backwards rather than forwards. So I was going home thinking of work, I was even waking up in the middle of the night thinking of work.

Guiding is a lot easier than mining! I took a really big drop in salary to come back here, but there's no stress. I live locally, over the other side of the valley, and walk two miles to work. I have retired now but they ask us back to help out, so I come back two to four days a week.

It's slightly different as a museum than it was as a mine. The coffee shop was an electrician's and the education centre was where they did repairs. My old locker is still there. The area that I have shown you is not the part where I worked. From 1973 we had a drift – where you can walk into the mine. If you look up the valley you can see trains; and just by that was a drift, and that's where we had the coalface. I was a young guy and we used to work what are called at the sharp end – those faces.

Some of the people we take around, they talk about their fathers and grandfathers with pneumoconiosis. In the early days the men would work in a wall of dust but as time went on things improved – you'd have water sprays, you'd have dust suppression. The airflow is checked, the volume is still checked. Saying that, some of the boys are still affected by this – I'm lucky I suppose that I'm not.

We're importing gas, electricity, coal, now. We were self-sufficient at one time and could be self-sufficient again. But personally I can't see the government going that way now. The only thing that proved the government wrong was Tower Colliery where the boys put their redundancy in and went for another 20 years, but that's politics and I don't want to get into politics. But some of the boys here will get very political. Sometimes as well you'll get a bit of a wind-up between NUM men and NACODS men, but that's all good.

Emigrant sailing ship

Ulster American Folk Park

'This space is full of character and requires little dressing to make it complement your wedding theme,' says National Museums Northern Ireland of the Ship and Dockside Gallery. 'You will dine against the backdrop of a replica early emigrant sailing ship. It is also possible to have costumed visitor guides mingle with your guests during and after dinner and perhaps do some storytelling before the wedding party boards the ship to the American side for a relaxing post-dinner walk while the evening entertainment sets up.' The replica ship can thus be there right at the start of a new life for couples, just as 'The Brig Union', on which the replica is based, was the start of a new life for many Irish emigrants to the United States in the 19th century.

'The American side' has 18th and 19th-century houses brought from the eastern United States and reconstructed on the site. These include a log cabin like those the early settlers would have used, and the actual Tennessee plantation house built by second-generation Irish immigrant and slave owner Francis Rogan in about 1825. After strolling there, wedding parties can cross back to Ulster, via the ship, for the dancing. 'The Irish side' has churches, a printing press and houses from the Northern counties of Ireland such as a tiny cabin from the Sperrin Mountains which is believed to have housed a family of 12 poor tenant farmers before the potato famine of the mid-19th century.

The Ulster American Folk Park also houses the Mellon Centre for Migration Studies and invites visitors to consult documents, and perhaps even find evidence of their ancestors, there.

Assistant curator Liam Corry explained why the museum had reconstructed the ship and outlined the journeys the original would have taken.

> The ship represents the transition from the Old World of Ireland to the New World of America. It's based on 'The Brig Union' which was built around 1810. We had details of families who lived where the Folk Park is today and emigrated to the United States in that boat (technically a ship has three masts while a brig would only have two), so we chose that one to replicate in the museum.
>
> The families who emigrated on 'The Brig Union' were related to the Mellon family, around whom our museum is built up. Their original cottage stands in the museum grounds today. The young Thomas Mellon was five years old when he left. He got a good education in the USA

and practised law before becoming a judge. After retiring he set up the T Mellon and Sons' Bank in 1869. This allowed the Mellon family to invest in small expanding companies of the time which went on to become household names in the oil, steel, electrical and aluminium industries. The bank is still in existence as the BNY Mellon, a huge merchant bank.

'The Brig Union' was involved in the timber trade bringing wood from Canada to Britain; on the return journey the hold would have been fitted out for steerage passengers as an alternative to ballast. Emigrants chose this route as it was cheaper than going directly to the USA. The journey back to Canada varied between 4 to 10 weeks. The families would then have travelled to the USA first by boat along the coast and then by wagon across land to frontier settlements along the Appalachian Mountains. Our families bought developed land near the frontier.

The design was taken from existing plans of brigs of the period but 'The Brig Union' plans or dimensions are not known for certain. The ship is 25 feet across the beam and is 66 feet long, but is truncated – it would be about 80 feet full length. This would be around average for a brig in the early 1800s. The steerage quarters would be actual size but with a bit more headroom; there might only have been 5 feet but we have slightly over 6 feet; people are taller now.

Huge numbers of people left Ireland for America from 1815 to 1914; every family would have branches in America even if now the links are being lost. 80% of Irish emigrants went to America in that timeframe. Emigration to Britain increased in the 1930s as the depression of that era was deeper in the USA than Britain. Then the Second World War came along and more Irish were attracted to work in the UK, plus there were no passenger ships to the USA. The 1950s and 60s saw good employment prospects in the UK and it was only the depression of the 80s that saw emigrants once again head for the USA in large numbers as illegals.

The replica ship allows visitors to get an idea of life on board; it is an immersive experience which allows them to get an idea of the cramped conditions. It also provides a transition in our story of emigration. Prior to the dockside scene we have a number of original houses brought into the museum with their unique family histories. After the transition through the hold of the vessel the visitor emerges into the New World part of the museum with its original American houses associated with Irish people.

In the hold of the boat there were originally the smells associated with a journey in such cramped conditions – they had to be removed after a few weeks of opening as they proved too strong for people to deal with. The sounds allow the mind to be carried away to a port, enhancing the visual experience on the ship and dock side.

American visitors whose ancestors left Ireland before the age of steam (1870 onwards) do consider what the voyage would have been like. Very few have actual stories from the time but it is an aid to them making a connection.

MONASTERBOICE CROSS

Victoria and Albert Museum, London

WALKING INTO A CAST COURT at the V&A is like entering a disorienting world of larger dimensions, in which you have suddenly shrunk. One court is crimson, one orange. In the crimson one, two huge columns stand in the centre like giant tree trunks (actually a cast of the Roman emperor Trajan's triumphal column from the first century AD, cut in half to fit it in). A full-size cathedral entrance with Christ, angels and apostles, is at one end of the room.

As you wander further, strange angles and juxtapositions reveal themselves. A lion's head appears through the arch of a choir screen; English 13th and 16th-century effigies sleep in their armour and robes next to a Norwegian doorway. Dramas emerge: a woman in a blindfold holding a broken spear turns away from another woman with a cup and a banner on a cross. The blindfolded woman is Synagogue, turning away from Ecclesia, the Christian church. Higher up, a muscular Perseus holds up Medusa's head, her body slumped at his feet, severed carotid arteries poking from her neck.

This mini-city of jumbled monuments opened in 1873. It is two enormous rooms stuffed full of plaster casts of statues, sculptures and buildings from Northern Europe, Spain and Italy. Casts were an essential part of educating designers, considered by the museum 'superior to drawings, as they render the whole treatment to the mind as palpably as possible'. So an aspiring 19th-century designer with no money for a grand tour of Europe could visit the Courts instead, to practise their trade by copying from the best. High up under the balustrade names of cities famous for their art history are painted in gold in alphabetical order – Paris, Pavia, Pegu, Persepolis; Salamanca, Salisbury, Seville.

The Monasterboice cross is a five and a half metre-high copy of the 10th-century original in the early Christian settlement of Monasterboice in County Louth in Ireland. Its surface is covered with reliefs of scenes from the Bible, figures from the Zodiac and other images which scholars cannot identify.

One person holds a guitar; others talk. A woman presents a baby to a queue of people while others stand in line in front of a leader or teacher. A Christ-like figure holds a cross and something which looks like a pair of scales. Two animals at the bottom might be fighting. The cast seems to have reproduced signs of wear on the original, so these people's features have been rubbed away, and the base is pockmarked and worn.

Chris Rose is a Science-Arts-Design consultant at Rhode Island School of Design. He has been visiting the Cast Courts for years, and here he looks closely at the cross for the first time. As he responds to it, he makes connections to many other things, and his uncertainty about the meaning of some of its scenes becomes a space for his imagination to work.

> The first thing I noticed walking towards this massive great object was that it has got a funny little roof on top of it, and when I looked closer I realised that it was a small building. So the shape of the cross could be almost like a garden spreading out in front of the house. There is all sorts of information packed into that area, all divided up into zones.
>
> I am really interested in certain aspects of Asian art such as Tibetan mandalas, mainly because they have a geometrical way of laying out information, and this seems to me to be using the idea of a map of the four cardinal points. It makes me think of one of the principal Tibetan Buddhist mandalas which is the Wheel of Cyclic Existence, and it uses a very similar compositional device. It reminded me too of going to a fruit market actually, because there are all these little

bobbly shapes packed into boxes and on an abstract level it has that effect.

It also reminded me, because these symbolic creatures are in the margins of this object, of a famous English illustrated manuscript called the Macclesfield Psalter that's in the Fitzwilliam Museum, and this has extraordinary Monty Python-type themes in these animals around the edges. And there are definitely two Egyptian-looking figures sitting at the bottom.

The curious thing about this cross is that it is such a massive impressive form, but it has these different kind of references. We've got people, animals, stories, events, we've got narratives, we've got possible sources of reference which are older or coming from elsewhere in the world, which I think is quite magical or mysterious, and it is all relating to this packed narrative composition. There is clearly a general theme of everything being interlocked together, a kind of social commentary about the interlocked nature of society linked to religious principles.

Anyway, coming back to the piece as a whole, I just love the idea that now I can see it as a house. The house is a very sacred form, it has everything flowing from that house, so it could be the house of God but it is also making a domestic and social reference to what is contained within human beings.

The Curious

IN THIS FINAL SECTION are three objects which featured in original cabinets of curiosity. Many objects from those early cabinets were lost, sold or destroyed. Others survive in today's museums, sometimes in recreations of the originals. The Basel Historical Museum in Switzerland, for example, has a *Wunderkammer* divided into Naturalia, Antiquitata, Artificialia and Scientifica, containing objects from the Amerbach family's 17th-century collection which started the museum in the 19th century.

For those collectors, curiosities were evidence of God's perfect design or even intervention in the natural world, or were the sole available evidence of far-flung places and people, or were evidence of wealth or knowledge to show visitors. Prudence Leith-Ross and Jennifer Potter, biographers of early collectors the Tradescants, point out that to be called 'curious' was a mark of social and intellectual distinction in the early 17th century, and meant that you were at the forefront of knowledge-gathering.

What can these objects offer us now, three hundred years after the last true cabinets of curiosity were formed? Today, studying objects is not a central source of knowledge for many of us or a skill taught outside disciplines such as archaeology, palaeontology or design. We have different ethical values too, and modern museum visitors may equate the acquisition of exotic and unusual objects with colonialism or even theft.

Each of the curiosities here has found a different afterlife. The first, from the collection of Hans Sloane, which started the British Museum, is a drawer of medical samples. In the British Museum it tells an early part of the story of the development of scientific thought during the Enlightenment. The lead curator of the Enlightenment Gallery explains that her team wanted visitors to look at objects through the eyes of those 16th and 17th-century collectors, and suggests how the design of the gallery helps people to do this.

We then look at an animal skin, tanned and decorated by Native American Indians, part of the collection acquired by Royal gardeners John Tradescant the elder and younger on their trips to Europe, North Africa, Russia and America in the 17th century. The collection in their Lambeth house was later to start Britain's first public museum, the Ashmolean. Their catalogue states that the skin belonged to Powhatan 'the king of Virginia', the father of Pocahontas. An educator at the Ashmolean talks about the object's second life in the gallery, helping schoolchildren to connect with other cultures.

Last is a Vegetable Lamb of Tartary. Sloane had at least one of these in his collection, as did the Danish physician and natural philosopher Ole Worm, and one was listed in the Tradescants' collection. It is not certain where this one comes from, but it is a prize exhibit in London's Garden Museum in St-Mary-at-Lambeth church, where the Tradescants lie buried. This object has a strong hold on people's imaginations and affections. A conservator describes her close relationship with it, and quotations from writers from the 17th to the 21st centuries show how the lamb continues to intrigue.

Hans Sloane's Specimen Tray

British Museum, London

THE SCENT OF WOOD POLISH is strong in the Enlightenment Gallery. Footsteps echo on the oak and mahogany floors as visitors walk its length, pausing over low wooden display cases or the packed wall cupboards. Beige stone pillars and white classical statues punctuate the room, under a mezzanine with gold railings. Friezes line the high ceiling. Busts of collectors Charles Townley and classical scholar Richard Payne Knight stand on tall plinths next to Clytie, who in Greek myth pined away for love of the sun god Apollo and was turned into a flower. She hangs her head sadly, one breast uncovered.

This room, also known as the King's Library because it was built for George III's books, is the oldest in the British Museum. It houses an exploration of ways that people thought about the world from the 1680s, when Hans Sloane started collecting, until the 1820s, when the room was completed. The gallery traces how the gathering and study of the earliest collections by British men and women led on to the development of scientific discovery during the Enlightenment.

You are invited to read and compare objects carefully. In the 'animals and shells' case three different ways of collecting are shown side by side. There are shells collected by Sloane from all over the world, reflecting his 'encyclopaedic' approach. Next to them are the Reverend Cracherode's large multi-coloured conches, collected for their beauty and rarity, like old master drawings. And next to those is Joseph Banks's more scientific collection made during Captain Cook's first voyage on the 'Endeavour' from 1768 to 1771.

You need to crouch down to view Sloane's specimen tray. In 49 little compartments lie muddy-coloured substances – boxes of powders, sorted stones and tiny objects in cork-stoppered cylinders. Substances in the tray include a skink (a type of lizard), a mummy's finger, which could be ground and used for bumps and bruises, and a piece of a skull with moss on it, thought to be a cure for the falling sickness (epilepsy).

Kim Sloan, as the Francis Finlay curator of the Enlightenment Gallery, led the curatorial team which planned it. She says why the tray and Sloane's collections remain important.

> Sloane probably collected many of these 'cures' out of historical interest rather than because they were still believed to work. Here we are on the cusp of a period when people are moving from superstitions and tradition based on Renaissance texts, to looking at things with the eyes of reason. The specimen trays are very good for showing and explaining that.
>
> Sloane's collections also tell us things that are relevant today, once we stop looking at them as curiosities and start studying them more scientifically. For example, in Sloane's herbarium, the albums of plant specimens in his collection, there are plants that are extinct, or that no longer grow in the places where they were originally found. Some of his artefacts also tell us about cultural practices which no longer happen today. Cultural groups which these artefacts came from can be quite surprised to see something from their past that is now forgotten.
>
> When we take students to the 'trade and discovery' area of the gallery the first word which often springs to their lips is 'loot'. But most of these objects were acquired through purchase, gift and trade. Understanding them as loot is a 20th or 21st-century concept. Understanding the historical context helps people get perspective.
>
> There is a subtle relationship between the floor cases and the wall cases that is probably missed by most visitors, but

the intention is that if they read the labels in the floor case, and look up, they will find more objects of the same type in the wall cases but with far fewer labels. So they will find themselves looking at the objects in the wall cases as though through 18th-century eyes – that is, they must compare and contrast and use deduction and reasoning, to understand what they are seeing – with about as much background knowledge about the objects as someone in the 18th century would have who had never encountered them before.

Some visitors may come away with simply a visual or sensory experience, and if people come out feeling they've been in a historical space then that is something. If they explore other parts of the museum but think of the Enlightenment Gallery as giving a context to other objects and the ways they were acquired and understood, then that's a bonus.

POWHATAN'S MANTLE

Ashmolean Museum of Art and Archaeology, Oxford

EXPLORER-GARDENERS John Tradescant the elder and younger collected plants and curiosities from around the world in the early 17th century. The elder piggybacked on diplomatic expeditions, first in 1618 with Sir Dudley Digges, sent to Archangel (then called Muscovy) by James I to negotiate a trading route through Russia to China and Persia. Then in 1620 he accompanied Robert Mansell on an expedition to Algeria to 'quell the Barbary pirates' – demand the return of captured English ships, goods and men. John Tradescant the younger travelled to America three times, the first trip in 1637.

The 'Ark to Ashmolean' gallery holds some of the curiosities collected on these trips, and plots the way the Ashmolean developed from their collection. Inside, the two men and Hester, the wife of the younger, gaze out solemnly from oil paintings on the walls. In the cases opposite them are objects including a Russian counting frame and 'Barbary Spurres pointed Sharp like a Bodkin' which John Tradescant the elder might have collected from North Africa (gallery labels are tentative about the origin of many of the objects, since the Tradescants did not record which expeditions particular objects belonged to). A bronze dodo sculpture stands in for the Tradescants' stuffed one, of which only a few remnants survive in storage.

North American objects in the collection include Virginian purses, a leather and shell pouch and wampum girdles. There is also a Canadian caribou skin tunic, listed in their 1656 catalogue; also listed were a 'Match-coat from Greenland of the intrails of fishes', 'a Portugall habit' and 'a Brackmans vest of Leaves of Aloes'.

Nearby a large piece of deerskin decorated with shells is laid out. This is known as the 'mantle' of Powhatan, father of Princess Pocahontas, who the Tradescants called 'King of Virginia'.

Archaeologist Giovanna Vitelli, Director of the Ashmolean's University Engagement Programme, talked about why the mantle might have been collected, and about how our view of it has changed since the Tradescants' time.

> 'Powhatan's Mantle', the caribou skin coat and the leather and shell pouch you can see here are some of the earliest North American ethnographic objects curated in museums today. It's a miracle they are still around. The mantle may have been a gift exchanged as part of a diplomatic process between English settlers and Chesapeake tribes.

The Tradescants aimed to bring together as many diverse objects and materials as possible so that through comparison of groups of objects, knowledge could be created about things and places that the era of exploration had opened up. North American objects and other objects from 'exotic' lands weren't any more or less prized than some of the other rarities that the Tradescants collected. They were placed in categories such as 'garments' or 'warlike instruments'. Powhatan's Mantle was catalogued along with Henry VIII's hawking gloves!

There are questions you can ask about it, even if you can't answer them. So for example, was some of the decoration meant to invest the mantle with personal or ritual meaning or value? What were the figures and symbols meant to convey? Women were undoubtedly involved in making it – in many cultures women dressed and decorated pieces of skin that men had hunted, so it would have been handed back and forth, so all members of the group would have contributed to something that symbolised their commitment to community.

We encounter it very differently now to the way someone might have done in the Tradescants' time. It's really interesting when you start to look at the experimental nature of knowledge creation in the 17th century. When you get these 'gentlemen scholars' around a table and they start to investigate cameos or mineral samples, what they have to do is experience them in order to build their knowledge and understanding of the materials they were observing. So they will pick it up, smell it, taste it – they were not squeamish about putting samples on the tongue – were they musty, were they acid? Their methods were sensual, tactile.

> In fact, early visitors to the museum often used to touch objects. The condition of the bottom third of the mantle suggests that it was within reach of a great many hands in the early days.

Education officer Clare Coleman has been working with schoolchildren at the Ashmolean for 10 years. She spoke about teaching schoolchildren with the mantle.

> We use Powhatan's mantle to explore native American Indian life and how they worked with natural resources–the mantle has beautiful shell decoration. It's very exciting for schoolchildren to see the real thing – we give them pieces of animal skin and also cowrie shells to touch while they are looking at it, which helps them to interpret it.
>
> When you are right next to it, the scale of it is impressive. It's like a Mona Lisa moment – when you see the Mona Lisa it's surprising how small it is. Here, it's amazing how big the mantle is. There is often one of those 'wow' moments when they first enter the gallery.
>
> The children become even more excited when they learn that the mantle belonged to Pocahontas's father. A colleague told me that a friend of hers didn't realise that Pocahontas was a real person until they saw the mantle in the Ashmolean.
>
> Working with objects can be more powerful than working with paintings. We can often relate more easily to objects as we may have used similar things. That way the museum objects become direct mediators between us and the makers.

THE VEGETABLE LAMB OF TARTARY

Garden Museum, London

THE GARDEN MUSEUM is in Saint Mary's Church near Lambeth Bridge on the Thames, a church site since the eleventh century, although now deconsecrated. In its graveyard lie five members of the Tradescant family. Also buried here is Vice-Admiral William Bligh, captain of 'The Bounty' when some of its crew famously mutinied in 1789, and later governor of New South Wales in Australia. Inside, beneath the stained glass and Gothic columns are pruning shears, bright pictures of gardens through the centuries, and books of horticulture. Delicious smells from the vegetarian café in the corner waft around the displays.

The lamb is one of the museum's treasures. It has a specially designed display case, the money donated by the family of a volunteer who, in the words of the museum's curatorial assistant Philip Norman, 'loved the old lamb'. A black and brown furry and slightly threadbare object, it is not easy to identify. It stands on its own island of dead vegetation, under a small glass cupola.

Vegetable lambs came from Central Asia, then known as Tartary, which included parts of modern day Siberia, Turkistan, Mongolia and China. People were said to believe that the lamb was both animal and vegetable. It was thought to be created by 'spontaneous generation' and attached to the earth by an umbilical cord. It had eyes, ears, hooves, blood and wool and died when it had eaten the grass around it. But many collectors did not believe this; for example, Hans Sloane identified it as a fern when he presented one to the Royal Society in 1698. And in fact vegetable lambs are dead ferns turned upside down and shaped so that the stalks, which grew upwards, become legs pointing downwards.

Sir Thomas Browne writes in *Pseudodoxia Epidemica*, his 17th-century work which aimed to investigate superstitions:

> Much wonder is made of the Baromez, that strange plant-animal or vegetable lamb of Tartary, which wolves delight to feed on, which hath the shape of the lamb, affordeth a bloody juyce upon breaking, and liveth while the plants be consumed about it... the Barometz is a union of animal and vegetable kingdoms.

But he goes on to warn that bees, flies and dogs can also be seen in plants and the lamb may therefore not be what it seems.

Others were also sceptical but were fascinated by how such a belief might have arisen. Writing in 1887, naturalist Henry Lee calls this 'a curious myth of the Middle Ages' and quotes John Bell, an early eighteenth century traveller, as saying 'after a careful enquiry of the more sensible and experienced among the Tartars, I found they regarded it as a ridiculous fable.' Lee was determined to get to the bottom of the story and proposed that the vegetable lamb was a cotton pod, and its fleece cotton wool.

Fiction writers have also long been fascinated by the lamb. Argentinian writer Borges, for example, includes the lamb in his Book of Imaginary Beings, remarking: 'other monsters are made up by combining various kinds of animals; the Barometz is a union of the animal and vegetable kingdoms.'

In his 2007 novel *Evolution* the science-fiction writer Stephen Baxter imagines a future world where the story of the lamb lives on: 'mankind's legends were forgotten now, but the tale of the Borametz... found strange echoes'. In this world, trees put out 'snaking umbilicals', which worm their way into the stomachs of the post-human inhabitants. The trees and post-humans thus form a symbiotic relationship; the trees deliver nutrients in their sap to post-humans, who in return tend the tree. But the tree rejects weaker specimens. A baby is born to a woman called Ultimate, and the tree decides it cannot afford to nurture the baby and starts to reabsorb her. The mother rescues her baby, pulling 'the belly-root from the infant's gut, and bits of white fibre from her mouth and nose'.

Are the pleasures that the lamb now offers similar to those it offered to collectors and travellers of the past, that of imagining how such a creature might feed and live, or how the myth arose? At any rate, it continues to play in people's imaginations.

Conservation student Sylvia Haliman worked on restoring the museum's lamb over a three-month period. She describes this task and talks about her relationship with the lamb. Intriguingly, her initial approach takes us back to when people asked themselves whether it was a plant or animal.

> The first thing we do is find out its material; that's fundamental. Was it a plant or animal? Looking at it, you wouldn't have guessed. It could have been a paw from an animal, for example, it was quite ambiguous. It didn't seem to be completely vegetable matter, because it's got that hair, like a fleece. When I showed it to course colleagues and a lecturer some people thought it was an artwork or flower arrangement.

> Another thing that attracted me is the fact that it is arranged – it looks a bit like taxidermy – it's got its own home, habitat, like a diorama setting, so I was quite intrigued by that. I tidied up the surrounding vegetation to stabilise it, and removed some pests – carpet beetles and vodka beetle larvae. I came to treat it like a living being. Because it's a biological object, it's probably still living... it's ageing. Usually an object is a functional object, or a working object, it's set its boundaries, but because this is so open, it's more intriguing.

The friend who first introduced me to the lamb used to come in regularly to see it. People may not know what it is or know much about its history and material, yet they are drawn to it – simply because it is quite enigmatic.

The most dangerous thing is if it's left forgotten or inaccessible. I want conservation to give greater access to the collections – and this is such a popular object, almost iconic, and it belongs to people who remember it fondly.

Conclusion:
Closing the Cabinet

THE CATEGORIES IN THIS BOOK have acted as holding grounds for the objects; a temporary way of organising and understanding them. But while writing it I found that the objects would suggest themselves for other categories, which drew different things from them. The Babylonian tablet, for example, (a document as much as an object) could well belong in 'the verbal' rather than 'the extinct'. This would lead to a closer focus on its cuneiform script, described as 'the world's oldest and hardest writing' by the speaker Irving Finkel, rather than the now extinct civilisation of which the tablet was part.

New categories also arose. One was for hybrid objects, containing the vegetable lamb (plant/animal), the mermaid leaflet (human/animal) and the statue of Lucifer (man/woman). These are all fictional or mythological in nature, and through them one could explore the peculiar attraction of hybrid objects, the puzzle they present and their ability or inability to offer new ways of understanding ourselves and the natural world. There are other intriguing categories awaiting investigation: the fake, the unidentified, the edible, the tiny. The reader may have their own.

So I would argue that categorisation and labelling can be creative activities, and ones which highlight the ways in which words and objects do not fit together perfectly. I found that it felt wrong if objects were treated as illustrations of one particular story. The Big Pit Museum, for example, is for the public authorities a cultural and financial asset and chance to strengthen Welsh identity; for the academic it is a place whose presentation as a World Heritage Site disguises local wealth inequality and environmental exploitation caused by mining; for the ex-miner who takes guided tours it is a workplace of which he has mixed memories, and which is now a congenial place of employment. Likewise, the euthanasia machine fits into neither pro- nor anti-euthanasia polemic for the visitor quoted in that section.

Of course, which aspects of objects are offered to us also depends on the 'mission' of the individual museums. For instance, exhibits are used at National Museums Liverpool to expose and deplore the fact that a great deal of the city's wealth was built on slavery. In contrast, slave-owning is mentioned without comment on the website of Ulster Museum and Folk Park, since it was practised by the son of an Irish emigrant who made good in the United States, whose house the museum has reconstructed.

Unexpected links between the objects arose; some significant, some no more than chance connections. The flood myth, parts of which were chipped into the Babylonian tablet between the fifth and seventh centuries BC, the story itself at least 1000 years old by that time, has worked its way through various filters to the Bibles used by modern Methodists worshipping under the Wesley monument outside the Museum of London in the 21st century. Genealogically, their god is the same as that of the Judaeans, who lived side by side with those Babylonians. Another connection is between Lucifer, who in the hands of ceramicist Matt Smith is an outsider to identify with, and Milton's portrayal of the fallen angel as anti-hero in *Paradise Lost*.

While writing the book I have been taken down many interesting byways too; when investigating mercury, for example, I have for the first time explored Muslim women's online forums, to read members discussing skin bleaching cream and telling each other to be happy with the skin colour Allah has given them. Mercury also led me to 'distressed mirrors' (surely another prime candidate for a modern day curiosity cabinet) which safely mimic the sparkly effect of old mirrors whose mercury-silver amalgam has deteriorated.

Such connections and explorations depend upon access to a wealth of information we take for granted today, often accessed with a click of a mouse, which was not available to early curiosity collectors. When John Tradescant the elder recorded in his diary the new roses he saw in Russia in 1618, he had no way to formally categorise or even name them, so that he had to match them in his mind with native species: 'they be single and muche like our sinoment [cinnamon] rose, and who have the sence of smelling say they be marvelus sweete. I hop they will both growe and beare heere [in England].' He subsequently gave these flowers a Latin name in his plant list and as his biographer Prudence Leith-Ross notes, nearly 40 years later his son was growing a *Rosa Moscovita*, so his hope may have been fulfilled.

The decline of curiosity cabinets

By the beginning of the 18th century many private curiosity collections had become part of more comprehensive, ordered collections which took an increasing role in publicly funded research and sometimes in public education. The solitary visitor studying and enjoying collections of curiosities at the invitation of their owners gave way to groups of people buying tickets to enter public galleries.

New scientific methodologies emerged along with the spread of new technologies such as the microscope. Naturally, most of the practical procedures and many of the intellectual ones required by modern empirically-based science were largely unknown or unavailable to the cabinet owners – striving for objective observation; recording exactly where specimens came from; dissecting specimens methodically, to give a few examples. Modern scientists usually need to investigate the typical, not the atypical, when trying to understand natural phenomena. When Elias Ashmole bequeathed the Tradescants' collection to Oxford University in 1677, he said 'for the knowledge of nature is requisite the inspection of particulars, especially those that are extraordinary in their fabric.' The first part of this sentence still holds; the second does not.

Nevertheless, that does not mean there are no links between cabinets and the later more scientific investigative methods of the Enlightenment. The binomial naming system the Tradescants used, for example in *Rosa Moscovita*, was a forerunner of the Linnean one used today. Linnaeus himself used Hans Sloane's plants, drawings and catalogue text to inform his ideas. Historian Wilma George takes the view that 17th-century zoological collections contributed information, but not ideas, to the later revolutionary changes in plant and animal classification. Sloane thought that the way he organised his specimens was important: 'The collection and accurate arrangement of these curiosities constituted my major contribution to the advancement of science,' he commented in a letter to the Abbé Bignon, librarian to Louis XIV of France, in about 1730. The sorting of objects in the cabinet was in fact the beginning of categorisation that has in turn produced separate disciplines such as art history, anthropology and natural history. Central contributions to this debate can be found in books written and edited by Arthur MacGregor, the world expert on cabinets of curiosity.

Another link is the motivations of curiosity collectors. The Tradescants' biographer Jennifer Potter argues that 'in spirit' their collections linked the Renaissance *Wunderkammer* with later more scientific collections. Part of this spirit is surely the urge to travel, collect and display which early collectors such as Sloane and the Tradescants shared with later ones, such as Joseph Banks, whose specimens did much to add to knowledge of the world during the Enlightenment. Some of Banks's specimens are in the British Museum's Enlightenment Gallery, and anyone wanting to investigate links, or lack of them, between curiosity collections and ones which came later could do much worse than study the displays in the gallery which, as Kim Sloan comments when talking about Hans Sloane's specimen tray, was set up partly to explore this question.

The curiosity cabinet today

What currency does the curiosity cabinet have today? One of its attractions is that it unites human impulses of delight and curiosity with examination of the natural world. In 1985 historian William Shupbach praised the 'wonder mingled with awe and gratitude' of early curiosity collectors, which he compared unfavourably with the 'icy touch of reason' of modern science. Recently though, the more emotionally compelling aspects of science have been increasingly emphasised by scientists and science popularisers such as Stephen Jay Gould, Brian Cox, and Richard Dawkins. Writers such as these foreground their own life stories and the feelings of curiosity and wonder which have fuelled their own discoveries or interpretations of other people's.

Connected with this sense of wonder is the wonderfully enticing language of many collectors, and of their catalogues. Among the late 16th and early 17th-century collection of Robert Cotton, which formed a founding collection of the British Museum, was mentioned the 'toung of a fish, which tyme hath converted into stone'. The phrase is a reminder of how special the process of fossilisation is, and how truly magical it must have seemed before processes which prevent decomposition were identified.

Curiosity displays remain popular, sometimes simply as a way of using unusual collections. Warrington Museum and Art Gallery, for example, remodelled its bird room in 2014 as such a cabinet, mixing intriguing objects together with minimal information. So 'a Henry VI groat discovered in a cow's stomach' is displayed next to a wallet made from a seal's flipper. It is 'an aesthetic celebration of all creatures great and small rather than of scientific enquiry,' wrote a reviewer approvingly, while noting the lack of context, such as no references to ecological or environmental issues. Other UK museums with original cabinets on display include Pallant House Gallery in Chichester and London's V&A.

Artists too are often enticed by the invitation to make connections between disparate objects which the cabinet of curiosity model offers, sometimes using this method to challenge the way museums classify and present knowledge. When sculptor Damien Hirst was invited to make installations for the Enlightenment Gallery in 2008, rather than focusing on the gallery's historical narrative, he described it in terms very like a cabinet of curiosities: 'a cornucopia of exciting things from both the natural and man-made world' and picked out intriguing objects: 'the display of 13th-century English tiles from Maxstoke Priory depicting souls entering Heaven and Hell... the detailed paper collages of plants by Mary Delany... the prehistoric stone axes'. The coloured skulls he installed, said the museum, were 'a dark, superstitious riposte to the Enlightenment concerns – reason, collection and classification – that surround them.' For a Tate Modern installation in 2009, artist Mark Dion organised groups of volunteers to dig up junk from the Thames, clean and organise it, and fill a cabinet with it. The gallery explained that one of his aims was to make viewers question the way in which modern museums classify their collections. Both of these artists used the idea of curiosities to undermine more systematic and scientifically-based ways of ordering collections, and the knowledge they offered, which arose during the Enlightenment.

Cabinets of curiosities are undoubtedly limited – and undoubtedly fascinating. One of my favourite comments on them is about the 17th-century collector Lodovico Moscardo whose museum in Verona, says historian Krzysztof Pomian, was 'a universe to which corresponded a type of curiosity no longer controlled by theology and not yet controlled by science'. In my experience as a museum educator, the cabinet's uncontrolled space appeals strongly not only to artists but to archaeology students, writers, and museum visitors in general. And I would add that today's museums still have something of the cabinet about them, being places where Buddhist statues may sit next to ancient coins, rock stars' shoes keep company with prehistoric fossils. I wonder if our museums will ever be able to completely shake off the shadow of their predecessor. I hope they do not.

References and Further Resources

Introduction

Bacon, Francis. (1594) *Gesta Grayorum or the History of the High and Mighty Prince Henry Who Reigned and Died 1594 Together with a Masque.* Michigan: Ann Arbor digital library production service.

Hooper-Greenhill, Eilean (1992) *Museums and the Shaping of Knowledge* London: Routledge.

Impey, Oliver and McGregor, Arthur (1985) (eds.) *The Origins of Museums: the Cabinet of Curiosities in 16th and 17th Century Europe.* Oxford: Clarendon Press. Particularly these chapters: George, Wilma 'Alive or Dead: Zoological Collections in the 17th Century' pp. 179-187; Hunter, Michael 'The Cabinet Institutionalised: The Royal Society's Repository and its Background' pp. 217-229; McGregor, Arthur 'The Cabinet of Curiosities in 17th Century Britain' pp. 201-215; Schupbach, William 'Some Cabinets of Curiosities in European Academic Institutions' pp. 169-178. The Francis Bacon quotation is from p. 1.

McGregor, Arthur (2007) *Curiosity and Enlightenment: Collectors and Collections from the 16th to the 19th Century.* New Haven: Yale University Press.

Pearce, Susan (1992) *Museums, Objects and Collections: a Cultural Study.* Leicester: Leicester University Press.

Pomian, Krzysztof. (1990) *Collectors and Curiosities.* Cambridge: Polity Press. The John Evelyn quotation is from p. 71.

Wilson, David (2002) *The British Museum: A History*. London: British Museum Press.

The comment about the Tradescant collection was made by merchant and traveller Peter Mundy. *The Travels of Peter Mundy* (1919) Hakluyt Society Vol 3 part (i).

The Touchable

Introduction

Classen, Constance (2007) 'Museum Manners: the Sensory Life of the Early Museum'. *Journal of Social History* 40 (4). The quotation from Celia Fiennes is from p.2 and from Sophie de la Roche p.8.

Quilt

Introduction to the quilt collection at the National Museum of Wales:
https://www.museumwales.ac.uk/rhagor/galleries/quilts/

'Academic quilter' Ann Rippin's blog:
https://annjrippin.wordpress.com

Bastet figurine

List of University College London's publications on the effect of handling museum objects on well-being:
http://www.ucl.ac.uk/museums/research/touch/publications

Data used in this section is taken from these articles:

Chatterjee, Helen; Vreeland, Sonjel and Noble, Guy (2009) 'Museopathy: Exploring the Healing Potential of Handling Museum Objects' *Museum and Society* 7 (3) pp. 164-177.

Lanceley, Anne; Noble, Guy; Johnson, Michelle; Balogun, Nyala; Chatterjee, Helen and Menon, Usha (2011) 'Investigating the Therapeutic Potential of a Heritage-Object Focused Intervention: a Qualitative Study' *Journal of Health Psychology*. Sage Publications.

Morse, N., Thomson, L.J., Brown, Z. & Chatterjee, H.J. (2015) Effects of creative museum outreach sessions on measures of confidence, sociability and well-being for mental health and addiction recovery service-users. *Arts & Health: An International Journal of research, Policy and Practice*, 7(3) pp. 231-246.

Thomson, Linda J.M., Ander, Erica E., Menon, Usha., Lanceley, Anne and Chatterjee, Helen (2012) 'Quantitative Evidence for Wellbeing Benefits from a Heritage-in-Health Intervention with Hospital Patients' *International Journal of Art Therapy: Formerly Inscape.* 17 (2) pp. 63-79.

Winnicott, Donald (1992) 'Transitional Objects and Transitional Phenomena' (first published in 1951) in *Through Paediatrics to Psychoanalysis: Collected Papers* pp. 229-242. London: Brunner-Routledge.

The UCL researchers have developed a 'toolkit' to help museums measure the effect of museum and gallery activities on participants' assessments of their own well-being, available here:
> https://www.ucl.ac.uk/museums/research/touch/ museumwellbeingmeasures/wellbeing-measures/ UCL_Museum_Wellbeing_Measures_Toolkit_Sept2013.pdf

Souvenir anointing spoon

Royal historic palaces online gift shop
> http://www.historicroyalpalaces.com/

The Recreated

Introduction

Benjamin, Walter 'The Work of Art in the Age of Mechanical Reproduction' (first published in 1955) in *Illuminations* (1999) (ed.) Hannah Arendt London: Pimlico pp. 211-244.

Casts of the Parthenon sculptures

Haydon, Benjamin *The Autobiography of Benjamin Robert Haydon* (1927) (ed.) Edmund Blunden. Oxford World's Classics Oxford: Oxford University Press. Quotations are from pp. 83, 85 and 108.

O'Keeffe, Paul (2009) *A Genius for Failure: the Life of Benjamin Robert Haydon* London: Bodley Head. The quotation about 'the muscle shown under one arm pit' is from p. 67.

Wall, John (2008) *That Most Ingenious Modeller: the Life and Work of John Henning, Sculptor 1771-1851* Ely: Melrose Books.

Henning's moulds and casts of the Parthenon sculptures are listed in the 'Highlights' section of the British Museum's 'Explore' database:
http://www.britishmuseum.org/explore.aspx

The Colossus rebuild

Open University video about Colossus, including an interview with Tony Sale:
http://www.youtube.com/watch?v=EdxBO9jfU8k

Tony Sale's site
http://www.codesandciphers.org.uk

Copeland, Jack and others (2010) *Colossus: The Secrets of Bletchley Park's Code Breaking Computers* Oxford: Oxford University Press.

Lucifer

Matt Smith's website
http://mattjsmith.com/

The Ephemeral

Introduction

The Museum of Brands, Packaging and Advertising:
http://www.museumofbrands.com/

Mermaid flyer

Rickards, Maurice (2000) *The Encyclopedia of Ephemera* London: The British Library; New York: Routledge.

Twyman, Michael (2008) 'The Long-Term Significance of Printed Ephemera' in *RBM: A Journal of Rare Books, Manuscripts, and Cultural History*, 9 (1) pp. 19-57.

Toilet paper

Miller, Daniel (2008) *The Comfort of Things* Cambridge: Polity Press.

Jonathan Fryer's Twitter feed

The UK Web archive
http://www.webarchive.org.uk/ukwa/

Jonathan Fryer on Twitter
http://www.webarchive.org.uk/ukwa/target/28475435/collection/100698/source/collection

The International Internet Preservation Consortium, which lists organisations aiming to archive the web:
http://netpreserve.org/

The Lethal

Introduction

Museum of Death, Los Angeles:
http://www.museumofdeath.net/info

Boehm, Mike 'Museum of Death in LA Buys Kevorkian Suicide Device Thanatron' *Los Angeles Times* July 21 2014.

Mercury

Stillman's (including a statement about the safety of its creams on the 'FAQs' page)
http://www.stillmans.com/products/

Gabler, Ellen and Roe, Sam 'Some Skin Whitening Creams Contain Toxic Mercury, Testing Finds', *Chicago Tribune* May 18 2010. Available online.

Gray, Theodore (2009) *The Elements: A Visual Exploration of Every Known Atom in the Universe* New York: Black Dog and Leventhal Publishers. The quotation about mercury is from p.185.

Flintlock pistols

Listed in Glasgow Museums' collections database:
http://collections.glasgowmuseums.com/index.html

Euthanasia machine

'Euthanasia: a Thing of the Past or Future?' (undated, anonymous) *Suzy B: The Voice of Pro-Life Women in Politics* blog:
http://www.sba-list.org/suzy-b-blog/euthanasia-thing-past-or-future

Devene, Frank (2002) 'An Interview with Philip Nitschke' *Quadrant* magazine 46 (10).

The Dead

Introduction

De Goncourt, Edmond, epigraph in a catalogue of his and his brother's collection of Far Eastern art (sold at auction in 1897), in *The Connoisseur* 182 (1973:77), quoted in Frederick Baekeland, 'Psychological Aspects of Art Collecting' in *Interpreting Objects and Collections* (1994) (ed.) Susan Pearce, p.218.

Jeremy Bentham's auto-icon

A picture of the auto icon rotating, from the very useful Bentham Project website:
http://www.ucl.ac.uk/Bentham-Project/who/autoicon/Virtual_Auto_Icon

Marmoy, C.F.A. 'The "Auto-icon" of Jeremy Bentham at University College London', *Medical History*, 2 (1958), pp. 77-86. Bentham's will is quoted on p.80; the jeering reference from the contemporary is quoted on p.83.

Richardson, R. and Hurwitz, B. 'Jeremy Bentham's Self-Image: an Exemplary Bequest for Dissection', *British Medical Journal*, 295 (July-Dec. 1987).

Both articles are available from:
https://www.ucl.ac.uk/Bentham-Project/who/autoicon

A list of Shirin Homann-Saadat's boxes:
http://www.shirin-homann-saadat.com/boxes.html

The Living

Introduction

The Horniman Museum's coral research project, including a video of coral spawning:
http://www.horniman.ac.uk/about/project-coral/

Beamish Open Air Museum's 'traditional experiences':
http://www.beamish.org.uk/traditional-experiences-at-beamish/

Magelssen, Scott (2007) *Living History Museums: Undoing History through Performance* Maryland: Scarecrow Press. The quotation is from pp. xx and xxi.

Leafcutter ants

Dawkins, Richard (2004) *The Ancestor's Tale: a Pilgrimage to the Dawn of Life* London: Weidenfeld and Nicolson. The quotation about ants is from p. 330.

The William Beebe tropical research station
http://www.wbtrs.org/

Darwin's weed garden

The American Museum of Natural History's online database of transcriptions of Darwin's manuscripts:
http://www.amnh.org/our-research/darwin-manuscripts-project

Darwin's letter to Joseph Hooker:
Darwin Correspondence Database,
http://www.darwinproject.ac.uk/entry-5835
This is an exceptionally well-designed and user-friendly database of digital transcriptions of Darwin's letters. It has many useful features including notes summarising each letter; biographies of each correspondent and links to further letters between them; and a keyword search facility.

Darwin, Charles (1868) *The Variation of Plants and Animals under Domestication* London: John Murray.

Darwin, Charles (1859) *On the Origin of Species* London: John Murray The quotation about seedlings is from p.80 of the illustrated edition ed. David Quammen (2008) New York: Sterling Publishing Co., Inc.

Captain Woodget

Live interpreter Andrew Ashmore's website:
http://ashmoreacts.org/

The Extinct

Introduction

Leakey, Richard and Lewin, Roger (1996) *The Sixth Extinction: Biodiversity and Its Survival* London: Weidenfeld and Nicolson. The quotation about the sixth extinction is from p. 254.

Manchester Museum's vivarium, with information about its frog conservation activities:
http://www.museum.manchester.ac.uk/collection/vivarium/

Code of Ethics for Museums (2008) London: Museums Association. Quotations about acquisition and care of objects and the environment from pp.14-19. Available from:
http://www.museumsassociation.org/ethics/code-of-ethics

'The Evacuation of Saint Kilda 29 and 30 August 1930' from the Glasgow Herald in *Scotland: the Autobiography* (ed.) Goring, Rosemary (2007) London: Viking p. 314.

Quagga skeleton

The Quagga Project
http://www.quaggaproject.org/

The Allan Wilson Centre, a New Zealand-based science organisation, has an intriguing web page, 'phylogenetic analysis of the quagga', which aims to take users through a similar series of steps to the scientists who sequenced the quagga's DNA.
http://www.allanwilsoncentre.ac.nz/

Harley, Eric; Lardner, Craig; Gregor, Michael; Wooding, Bernard and Knight, Michael H (2010) 'The Restoration of the Quagga; 24 years of selective breeding' in *Restoration of Endangered and Extinct Animals* Poznan: Poznan University of Life Sciences Press.

Heywood, Peter (undated) 'The Quagga and Science' available from the 'What's New' page of the Quagga Project website.

Higuchi R, Bowman B, Freiberger M, Ryder OA, Wilson AC (1984). 'DNA sequences from the quagga, an extinct member of the horse family'. *Nature* 312 (5991): 282-4.

Babylonian map of the world

Finkel, Irving (2014) *The Ark before Noah* London: Hodder and Stoughton.

The tablet has a detailed entry in the British Museum's 'research' database:
   http://www.britishmuseum.org/research.aspx
       (Search using the tablet's museum number: 92687)

Bends for peat flittin'

Website
   http://www.fetlar.org/

Flittin' Peats in Fetlar: A Photographic History (1994) Fetlar: Fetlar Interpretive Centre

The Mobile

Introduction

Videos of the spinning Egyptian statue in Manchester Museum can be found online.

The Verbal

Introduction

Berger, John (1972) *Ways of Seeing* London: Penguin. Quotations from pp. 20 and 21.

Bitgood, S., and Cleghorn, A. (1994) 'Memories of Objects, Labels and Other Sensory Impressions from a Museum Visit'. *Visitor Behaviour* 9 (2), 11-12.

McManus, Paulette (1989) 'Oh, Yes, They Do: How Museum Visitors Read Labels and Interact with Exhibit Texts' *Curator* 32 (3) pp 174-189.

Paradise Lost

Milton, John (2003) *Paradise Lost: a Poem in 12 Books* London: The Folio Society. Paradise Lost first published 1667.

Thomas Leyland's will

The account books for Leyland's ships *Hannah* and *Jenny* have been summarised online by Philip Heslip for the William L Clements library, University of Michigan:
   http://quod.lib.umich.edu/c/clementsmss/

Falconbridge, Alexander (1788) *An Account of the Slave Trade on the Coast of Africa* London: J Phillips. Available online.

Morgan, K. (2008) *Records Relating to the Slave Trade from the Liverpool Record Office: an introduction*,
   http://www.britishonlinearchives.co.uk/guides/9781851171477.php
         Last updated: 29 September 2008.

Dresser, M. and Hann, A. (2013) *Slavery and the British Country House* London: English Heritage.

The Domestic

Introduction

Bishop, Elizabeth 'Crusoe in England' in *Poems* (2011) (ed.) Saskia Hamilton New York: Farrar, Straus and Giroux.

Homemaker plate

Moss, Simon *Homemaker: a 1950s Design Classic* (1997) Moffat: Cameron & Hollis.

Homemaker tableware can be found in the V&A's 'search the collections' database:
   http://collections.vam.ac.uk/ (from where the quotation comes)

Woolworths virtual museum, with pictures of Homemaker displays: http://woolworthsmuseum.co.uk/1950s-i-chinaglass.htm

Gillian Carson's gardening blog: http://mytinyplot.com/vintage-seed-catalogues/my-lovely-homemaker-collection/

Claire Smyth's retro blog: http://theworldofkitsch.com/worldofkitsch/ridgway-homemaker-plate

Purbrick, Louise (2007) *The Wedding Present: Domestic Life Beyond Consumption* Aldershot: Ashgate.

The Mass Observation Archive which Purbrick used for her research into wedding presents. It is open access: http://www.massobs.org.uk/

Jane Austen's writing table

Austen-Leigh, Edward (2002) *A Memoir of Jane Austen* ed Kathryn Sutherland Oxford: Oxford World Classics. The quotation is from p.81. First published in 1870.

Jones, Cindy (2011) *My Jane Austen Summer* New York: HarperCollins

Tomalin, Claire (2000) *Jane Austen: a Life* London: Penguin.

Tomalin, Claire (2008) *Writers' Rooms: Jane Austen* The Guardian Saturday 12 July 2008.

The Huge

Big Pit National Coal Museum

Hoskins, Gareth (2014) 'The Spoils of Exploitation: Mining Museums' in *Planet: the Welsh Internationalist* 213 (spring 2014) pp. 40-51.

The Monasterboice cross

Baker, Malcolm (1982; revised 2007) 'The History of the Cast Courts': http://www.vam.ac.uk/content/articles/t/the-cast-courts/

The Curious

Introduction

Basel Historical Museum
 http://www.hmb.ch/en/programm

Powhatan's mantle

Potter, Jennifer (2006) *Strange Blooms: the Curious Lives and Adventures of the John Tradescants* London: Atlantic Books.

Leith-Ross, Prudence (1985) *The John Tradescants: Gardeners to the Rose and Lily Queen* London: Peter Owen publishers. Includes a transcription of John Tradescant the elder's journal from his trip to Russia in 1618.

Musaeum Tradescantium or: A Collection of Rarities Presented at South Lambeth near London by John Tradescant (1656) printed by John Grismond. The catalogue of the Tradescants' curiosities, compiled by John Tradescant the younger.

The Ashmolean Museum has an excellent section on its website devoted to the Tradescants' lives and work, including quotations from their catalogue:
 http://www.ashmolean.org/ash/amulets/tradescant/
  tradescant00.html

The Vegetable Lamb of Tartary

Baxter, Stephen (2007) *Evolution* London: Gollancz. Quotations are from p. 630 onwards.

Bondeson, Jan (1999) *The Feejee Mermaid and Other Essays in Natural and Unnatural History* Ithaca: Cornell University Press.

Borges, Jorge Luis (2002) *The Book of Imaginary Beings* (first published in 1967) London: Vintage Classics.

Browne, Thomas (1986) *Pseudodoxia Epidemica* (first published in 1646-1672). (ed.) Robbins, Robin. Oxford: Oxford University Press.

Lee, Henry (1887) *The Vegetable Lamb of Tartary: a Curious Fable of the Cotton Plant* London: Sampson Low, Marston, Searle and Rivington.

Conclusion

McGregor, Arthur 'The Cabinet of Curiosities in 17th Century Britain' pp. 147-158 in Impey, Oliver and McGregor, Arthur (1985) (eds.) *The Origins of Museums: the Cabinet of Curiosities in 16th and 17th Century Europe.* Oxford: Clarendon Press. The quotation about the 'toung of a fish' is from Impey and MacGregor p. 148, taken from pp.107 and 108 of *Original Letters of Eminent Literary Men of the 16th, 17th and 18th Centuries* (1843) (ed.) Ellis, William.

Pomian, Krzysztof. (1990). *Collectors and Curiosities.* Cambridge: Polity Press.

Schupbach, William 'Some Cabinets of Curiosities in European Academic Institutions' in Impey, Oliver and McGregor, Arthur (1985) (eds.) *The Origins of Museums: the Cabinet of Curiosities in 16th and 17th Century Europe.* Oxford: Clarendon Press. pp. 169-178. The quotation about the 'icy touch of reason' is from page 170.

'Cabinet of Curiosities, Warrington Museum', review by Sara Holdsworth. *Museums Journal*, 1 July 2014. pp 44-47.

Damien Hirst's comments can be found in 'Statuephilia' in the British Museum website archive of past exhibitions:

http://www.britishmuseum.org/the_museum/museum_in_london/london_exhibition_archive/statuephilia/damien_hirst.aspx

The Tate Thames dig and resulting cabinet display are documented in Tate Modern's online learning resources

List of Museums

Ashmolean Museum of Art and Archaeology
Beaumont Street
Oxford OX1 2PH
http://www.ashmolean.org/

Big Pit National Coal Museum
Blaenafon
Torfaen NP4 9XP
http://www.museumwales.ac.uk/bigpit/

Birmingham Museum and Art Gallery
Chamberlain Square
Birmingham B3 3DH
http://www.birminghammuseums.org.uk/bmag

Booth Museum of Natural History
194 Dyke Road
Brighton BN1 5AA
http://brightonmuseums.org.uk/booth/

Brighton Museum and Art Gallery
Royal Pavilion Gardens
Brighton BN1 1EE
http://brightonmuseums.org.uk/brighton/

The British Library
96 Euston Road
London NW1 2DB
http://www.bl.uk/

British Museum
Great Russell Street
London WC1B 3DG
http://www.britishmuseum.org

Centre for Ephemera Studies
Department of Typography & Graphic Communication,
University of Reading
2 Earley Gate
Whiteknights
Reading RG6 6AU
https://www.reading.ac.uk/typography/research/typ-researchcentres.aspx

Cole Museum of Zoology
Whiteknights
University of Reading
Reading RG6 6UA
https://www.reading.ac.uk/colemuseum/

Cutty Sark Clipper Ship
King William Walk
Greenwich
London SE10 9HT
http://www.rmg.co.uk/cuttysark

Down House
Luxted Road
Downe
Kent BR6 7JT
http://www.english-heritage.org.uk/visit/places/home-of-charles-darwin-down-house/

Elgin Museum
1 High Street
Elgin IV30 1EQ
http://www.elginmuseum.org.uk

Fetlar Interpretive Centre
Beach of Houbie
Fetlar
Shetland ZE2 9DJ
http://www.fetlar.com/index.htm

Garden Museum
Lambeth Palace Road
London SE1 7LB
http://www.gardenmuseum.org.uk/

Grant Museum of Zoology
Rockefeller Building
University College London
21 University Street
London WC1E 6DE
http://www.ucl.ac.uk/museums/zoology

The Helicopter Museum
Locking Moor Road
Weston-super-Mare
Somerset BS24 8PP
http://www.helicoptermuseum.co.uk/

International Slavery Museum
3rd Floor of Merseyside Maritime Museum
Albert Dock
Liverpool L3 4AX
http://www.liverpoolmuseums.org.uk/ism/

Jane Austen's House Museum
Chawton
Alton
Hampshire GU34 1SD
http://www.jane-austens-house-museum.org.uk/

Kelvingrove Art Gallery and Museum
Argyle Street
Glasgow
G3 8AG
http://www.glasgowlife.org.uk/museums/kelvingrove/Pages/default.aspx

Land of Lost Content
Market Street
Craven Arms
Shropshire SY7 9NW
http://www.lolc.org.uk/

Liverpool World Museum
William Brown Street
Liverpool
Merseyside L3 8EN
http://www.liverpoolmuseums.org.uk/wml/index.aspx

Milton's Cottage
Deanway
Chalfont Saint Giles
Buckinghamshire HP8 4JH
http://www.miltonscottage.org/

Museum of English Rural Life
University of Reading
Redlands Road
Reading RG1 5EX
https://www.reading.ac.uk/merl/

Museum of London
150 London Wall
London EC2Y 5HN
http://www.museumoflondon.org.uk/

The National Museum of Computing
Block H
Bletchley Park
Milton Keynes MK3 6EB
http://www.tnmoc.org/

Petrie Museum of Egyptian Archaeology
University College London
Malet Place
London WC1E 6BT
http://www.ucl.ac.uk/museums/petrie

Science Museum
Exhibition Road
London SW7 2DD
http://www.sciencemuseum.org.uk/

St Fagans Museum
St Fagans National History Museum
Cardiff CF5 6XB
http://www.museumwales.ac.uk/stfagans/

Ulster American Folk Park
2 Mellon Road
Omagh BT78 5QU
http://www.nmni.com/uafp

Ulster Museum
Botanic Gardens
Belfast
County Antrim BT9 5AB
http://nmni.com/um

University College London
Gower Street
London WC1E 6BT
http://www.ucl.ac.uk/Bentham-Project/who/autoicon

Victoria and Albert Museum
Cromwell Road
London SW7 2RL
http://www.vam.ac.uk/

Whipple Museum of the History of Science
Free School Lane
Cambridge CB2 3RH
http://www.hps.cam.ac.uk/whipple/

Acknowledgements

THANK YOU first of all to everyone who agreed to be interviewed for this book; it has been a privilege to listen to so many different people talking thoughtfully and enthusiastically, in many cases doing their best to summarise their life's work in a very short time. Thank you to family and friends for continual encouragement and comment, especially my mother Yvonne. Time and space at Martin, Fran and Emma Reynolds's finca in Spain enabled me to write the book. My friends in the Fiction Forge online writing group, particularly Valerie Waterhouse, have been constantly helpful. Early and late encouragement was given by Kate Dorney, Elizabeth Lyon, Louise Purbrick, Matt Smith, Rhi Smith and many others. Martha Fleming kindly reviewed the introduction and conclusion. All remaining mistakes are my own.

Working for the Centre for Excellence in Teaching and Learning through Design (CETLD) from 2006 to 2010 gave me a chance to explore questions about museums within the weird, enormous, enchanting and intimidating space which is the Victoria and Albert Museum in London. The Museum of English Rural Life, Reading has been an extremely supportive and stimulating workplace; thank you to all staff there.

Copyright and Permissions

Grateful acknowledgement is made to the following for permission to use extracts from these works:

Interview with Chris Rose about the Monasterboice Cross: © CETLD Centre for Excellence in Teaching and Learning through Design, Faculty of Art and Architecture, University of Brighton.

'The Evacuation of Saint Kilda 29 and 30 August 1930' © The Glasgow Herald.

Interview with Joan Coutts: © 1994 Fetlar Interpretive Centre.

Lanceley, Anne; Noble, Guy; Johnson, Michelle; Balogun, Nyala; Chatterjee, Helen and Menon, Usha (2011) 'Investigating the Therapeutic Potential of a Heritage-Object Focused Intervention: a Qualitative Study' *Journal of Health Psychology.* © Sage Publications.

Evolution by Stephen Baxter © 2007 The Orion Publishing Group Ltd.

Drawings are based on photographs with these copyrights: Tiller-Clowes troupe/ © Victoria and Albert Museum, London; pistols © Glasgow Museums; crocodile handbag © University of Reading; Big Pit © National Museum Wales; euthanasia machine © Science Museum; Babylonian tablet © British Museum; Lucifer © Birmingham Museum and Art Gallery.

Flintlock pistols
Kelvingrove Art Gallery and Museum

About the Author

Rebecca Reynolds is a teacher, writer and museum education consultant. Her main places of museums work have been the Victoria and Albert Museum, London and the Museum of English Rural Life, Reading. The core of her work is helping to make collections accessible to all, and developing creative and innovative ways of exploring them. She blogs about objects here:

http://objects-ofinterest.blogspot.com

About the Artist

Minho Kwon trained as an illustrator at the Royal College of Art in London and worked as an artist and lecturer at the Paju Typography Institute in Gyeonggi-do, South Korea, before becoming a freelance artist.

Printed in Great Britain
by Amazon